W9-BTF-052

EMILIANO ZAPATA

EMILIANO ZAPATA

A Biography

Albert Rolls

GREENWOOD BIOGRAPHIES

 GREENWOOD

AN IMPRINT OF ABC-CLIO, LLC
Santa Barbara, California • Denver, Colorado • Oxford, England

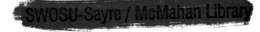

Copyright 2011 by Albert Rolls

Library of Congress Cataloging-in-Publication Data

Rolls, Albert.
  Emiliano Zapata : a biography / Albert Rolls.
      p. cm. — (Greenwood biographies)
  Includes bibliographical references and index.
  ISBN 978-0-313-38080-8 (hardcopy : alk. paper) — ISBN 978-0-313-38081-5
(ebook)   1. Zapata, Emiliano, 1879–1919.   2. Revolutionaries—
Mexico—Biography.   3. Mexico—History—Revolution, 1910–1920.
4. Mexico—Politics and government—1910–1946.   I. Title.
  F1234.Z37R65   2011
  972.08'1092—dc22   [B]   2011013272

ISBN: 978-0-313-38080-8
EISBN: 978-0-313-38081-5

15 14 13 12 11   1 2 3 4 5

This book is also available on the World Wide Web as an eBook.
Visit www.abc-clio.com for details.

Greenwood
An Imprint of ABC-CLIO, LLC

ABC-CLIO, LLC
130 Cremona Drive, P.O. Box 1911
Santa Barbara, California 93116-1911

This book is printed on acid-free paper ∞

Manufactured in the United States of America

CONTENTS

vi   CONTENTS

SERIES FOREWORD

In response to high school and public library needs, Greenwood developed this distinguished series of full-length biographies specifically for student use. Prepared by field experts and professionals, these engaging biographies are tailored for high school students who need challenging yet accessible biographies. Ideal for secondary school assignments, the length, format and subject areas are designed to meet educators' requirements and students' interests.

Greenwood offers an extensive selection of biographies spanning all curriculum-related subject areas including social studies, the sciences, literature and the arts, history and politics, as well as popular culture, covering public figures and famous personalities from all time periods and backgrounds, both historic and contemporary, who have made an impact on American and/or world culture. Greenwood biographies were chosen based on comprehensive feedback from librarians and educators. Consideration was given to both curriculum relevance and inherent interest. The result is an intriguing mix of the well known and the unexpected, the saints and sinners from long-ago history and contemporary pop culture. Readers will find a wide array of subject choices from fascinating crime figures like Al Capone to

inspiring pioneers like Margaret Mead, from the greatest minds of our
time like Stephen Hawking to the most amazing success stories of our
day like J. K. Rowling.

While the emphasis is on fact, not glorification, the books are meant
to be fun to read. Each volume provides in-depth information about
the subject's life from birth through childhood, the teen years, and
adulthood. A thorough account relates family background and education, traces personal and professional influences, and explores struggles,
accomplishments, and contributions. A timeline highlights the most
significant life events against a historical perspective. Bibliographies
supplement the reference value of each volume.

PREFACE

Denounced as a bandit and called the Attila of the South during the Mexican Revolution early in the 20th century, Emiliano Zapata was later made, by an act of the Mexican legislature, an official national hero and came to be regarded as one of Mexico's most notable 20th-century figures. The anniversary of his death is a day of national mourning, "an occasion for speeches celebrating Zapata's revolutionary career and presidential pronouncements on agrarian matters."[1] Such celebrations seem counter to the spirit of Zapata's life and of the post-revolutionary political system, which, after all, never fully supported the ideals for which Zapata fought. More recent moves to deemphasize his place in Mexican history in state-approved textbooks seem to provide a more genuine acknowledgment of who Zapata was, that is, a man who was willing to risk marginalization for the sake of struggling for what he believed was right. "As a national symbol Zapata connotes social justice," the scholar Emily Hind explains. He sought the return of land taken by wealthy landowners "to landless Mexicans," and in this respect, "the rhetoric of the official history was in tension with the [government's] neglect of rural issues."[2]

More interested in what he was fighting for than he was in personal
gain, Zapata is among the most conscientious examples of a revolutionary that one is likely to encounter in history. In the face of a victory that could have brought wealth to him rather than collective
justice to the people of Morelos—his home state—he kept fighting
for the agrarian reforms he took up arms to achieve, proving a counter
example to conventional rebels, who are, as the writer David Foster
Wallace remarks, "Great at exposing and overthrowing corrupt hypo-
critical regimes but . . . noticeably less great at the mundane, non-
negative task of then establishing a superior governing alternative.
Victorious rebels, in fact, seem best at using their . . . rebel-skills to
avoid being rebelled against themselves—in other words, they just become better tyrants."[3]

Zapata refused to profit from tyranny or to accept it, and that was
what impressed his followers the most. Rosa King, an English woman
who ran the Bella Vista, a resort hotel in Cuernavaca, recalled discussing Zapata with local women in the revolution's later years. Combining
a mixture of truth and rumor, King captures the importance of Zapata
to those for whom he fought.

> I told them, in my turn, what I had heard in Mexico City, that
> there was no leader in Mexico so popular as Zapata, since all men
> knew that he fought not for his own gain, but only "that there
> might be the same laws for the poor man as for the rich." . . . and
> that when he was in the capital the people would have made him
> president, but he would not let them, saying he was not the man
> for the place. . . . Their shrewdness told them that no man could
> walk wisely among matters he did not understand, and it was for
> this that they despised the Federal generals sent out to them. It
> was, I sensed, the essence of their trust in Zapata that he stayed
> close to the soil of his *tierra*, whose needs were part of him; es-
> chewing honors and wealth, . . . like a holy person dedicated to
> the service of his people, perhaps.

Even some of those who could not see beyond his contemporaries'
characterization of him as an outlaw acknowledged his honorable
intentions. In her memoir of the period, Leone B. Moats, for exam-

ple, condemns Zapata as a bandit and then, in the same paragraph, notes, "Throughout his career Zapata stuck to one cause, one quarrel. 'Land for the Indian!' that was all. He would fight for any one [sic] who promised that, then fight against them when, in power, they reneged."[4]

Moats's characterization of Zapata, while not inaccurate, simplifies the position in which he often found himself. Zapata did fight every major leader—Francisco Ignacio Madero, General Victoriano Huerta, and Venustiano Carranza—who took control of Mexico's government between 1910 and 1919, and while he played an instrumental role in helping each of them take power, the help he provided was not always that of an ally. The only revolutionary leader whom Zapata explicitly fought to put into power was Madero, whom he took up arms against once it became clear that land reform was low on the list of the new government's priorities.

Huerta's ability to take the presidency may have been aided by Zapata's rebellion against Madero, if only because the *Zapatista* opposition added to the political instability that allowed Huerta to rise to power, but the two generals were enemies from the start. Huerta had fought to repress the element of the *Maderista* movement that Zapata controlled after Madero succeeded in pushing Porfirio Díaz, the Mexican dictator whom the revolution first set out to overthrow, from office. Thus, when Huerta became Mexico's president, Zapata's fight continued without pause. The name of the enemy leader had simply changed.

Zapata's relationship to Carranza differed from his relationship to both Madero and Huerta. Carranza and Zapata were allies by default rather than choice. They fought independently, along with Pancho Villa, whose alliance with Carranza was more formal, to bring down Huerta, but their aspirations for the revolution differed. Carranza failed to see the need for radical social reform, regarding the struggle as a means to put more acceptable politicians in the positions held by those belonging to the former regime. Zapata thus distrusted Carranza from the start and opposed placing him in the presidential office after Huerta's government collapsed. Once Carranza assumed the presidency, Zapata continued his resistance, attempting to maintain the agrarian reforms that the *Zapatistas* had instituted in Morelos between Huerta's fall from and Carranza's rise to power.

Carranza proved Zapata's last enemy. A strong, coherent national opposition failed to materialize after 1917, the year that Mexico's new constitution was approved, and the *Zapatistas* were beset by a number of setbacks, including defections and illnesses. Zapata's last struggle to establish "a superior governing alternative," one that would be true to his ideals, was doomed to failure, and near the end, he came to understand that victory might only be possible through compromise. Determined to hold the strongest position possible at the negotiating table when such compromises would be made, he worked at forging alliances and attempted to rebuild his faltering movement. These efforts gave Carranza's forces an opportunity to gain the upper hand, trapping Zapata in an ambush that would put an end to his life but not the cry for Land and Liberty among those who looked to him for hope.

NOTES

1. Dennis Gilbert, "Emiliano Zapata: Textbook Hero," *Mexican Studies/Estudios Mexicanos* 19, no. 1 (Winter 2003), 128.

2. Emily Hind, "Historical Arguments: Carlos Salinas and Mexican Women Writers," *Discourse* 23, no. 2 (Spring 2001), 96.

3. David Foster Wallace, "E Unibus Pluram," in *A Supposedly Fun Thing I'll Never Do Again* (New York: Little Brown, 1997), 67.

4. Leone B. Moats, *Thunder in Their Veins: A Memoir of Mexico* (New York: Century, 1932), 82.

TIMELINE: EVENTS IN THE LIFE OF EMILIANO ZAPATA

c. 1879   c. August 8: Emiliano Zapata Salazar is born to Gabriel Zapata and Cleofas Salazar in Anenecuilco, Morelos, Mexico.

c. 1886   Sent to a local school in Villa de Ayala.

c. 1888   Anenecuilco's last orchard is seized by a local hacienda.

1897   Arrested by local police. He dated the beginning of his serious opposition to the haciendas in this year.

1906   April 15: Zapata takes part in a meeting with Morelos's governor to discuss the haciendas' appropriation of communal land surrounding Anenecuilco.

1906   Pablo Torres Burgos and Otilio Montaño settle near Anenecuilco and begin expanding Zapata's political education. Zapata's first son, Nicolás, is born to Inés Aguilar.

1908   Flees Morelos to escape facing local authorities.

1909   January 24: Joins the Melchor Ocampo Club, a Leyvista club supporting the opposition candidate in the 1909 gubernatorial election in Morelos.

1909   February 7: Pablo Escandón is elected governor of Morelos.

1909   May: Francisco Ignacio Madero forms the *Centro Anti-reeleccionista de Mexico* (the Anti-Reelectionist Party) to oppose Porfirio Díaz, Mexico's dictator, in the 1910 presidential election.

1909   September 12: Elected the president of Anenecuilco's village council.

1910   February 11: Begins his stint in the army in Cuernavaca.

1910   March: Having been discharged from the army with the help of Ignacio de la Torte y Mier, Díaz's son-in-law and Morelos's federal deputy, Zapata begins working in Ignacio's stables as chief groom in Mexico City.

1910   April: Madero is nominated as the presidential candidate for the *Centro Anti-reeleccionista de Mexico*.

1910   Begins to distribute land among the peasants, at first in Anenecuilco, but later in Villa de Ayala and Moyotepec as well.

1911   March 11: Joins the *Maderista* revolution, neutralizing, along with Torres Burgos and others, Villa de Ayala's police force. The group proceeds to gather recruits and heads to southern Puebla. By the end of the month, Torres Burgos quits the revolution and is killed by federal troops. Zapata is voted in as the revolutionary force's new leader.

1911   May 19: Zapata's forces successfully take Cuautla. Two days later, Díaz signs the Treaty of Ciudad Juarez, admitting defeat, and on May 25, he officially resigns and goes into exile.

1911   June 7: Meets Madero.

1911   June 22: Tells reporter that he is retiring from revolutionary activities.

1911   August 9: Marries Josefa Espejo in a religious ceremony; on the same day, General Victoriano Huerta arrives in Morelos to force the disarmament of Zapata's men.

1911   September 1: Forces loyal to the provisional revolutionary government attack Zapata for the first time, giving rise to Zapata's independent revolution. *Zapatismo* is born.

1911   November 6: Madero's presidential inauguration takes place.

1911   November 25: The Plan de Ayala is issued in Morelos: it would not be published in a national newspaper until December 15.

1912   January: Francisco Naranjo, Jr., becomes governor of Mo-
       relos. Shortly thereafter Brigadier General Juvencio Robles
       arrives in the state and institutes a policy of resettlement.

1912   November 1: The *Zapatistas* decide to finance their revolu-
       tion through taxing haciendas, the fields of which would
       be burned if the landowners refused to pay.

1913   February 9: A 10-day coup, which came to be known as the
       Decena Tragica (the Tragic Ten) begins, and on February
       19, Huerta is sworn into office as the new president.

1914   March 15: Zapata begins the siege of Chilpancingo, Guer-
       rera's state capital. After a week of fighting, the town falls,
       and later in the year, allies of Zapata establish their control
       of the state. The *Zapatistas* establish control over Morelos
       during the same period.

1914   July 15: Huerta resigns his presidency and goes into exile.
       Thereafter, *Zapatistas* consolidate their control over More-
       los and maintain it for more than a year.

1914   August 20: Venustiano Carranza assumes the position of
       First Chief of Mexico.

1914   October 27: *Zapatista* delegates arrive in Aguascalientes to
       join the convention that would lead to the formation of
       the Conventionist government.

1914   November 26: Zapata enters Mexico City, two days after
       his forces begin their occupation of the city. He quickly
       leaves, arriving back in Cuernavaca three days later.

1914   December 4: Meets Pancho Villa at Xochimilco, where
       their alliance is solidified. Two days later Zapata and Villa
       parade their troops through Mexico City.

1915   January 28: The Conventionist government relocates to
       Cuernavaca. The Convention would return to Mexico
       City on March 15.

1915   October: The United States gives de facto recognition to
       Carranza's government, forbidding arms to be sold to other
       revolutionary factions within Mexico. The *Zapatista* ele-
       ment of the Convention, nonetheless, establishes a shadow
       government in Cuernavaca.

1916   March 13: Francisco Pacheco effectively defects to the
       Carrancistas, allowing Carranza's forces to enter Morelos

and establish control over the state, and Zapata becomes little more than a fugitive, relying on guerrilla tactics to keep *Zapatismo* alive.

1917   January/February: The *Carrancistas* are completely driven from Morelos, leaving Zapata in control of the state once again. The victory would be Zapata's last. *Zapatismo* would experience little but decline over the next two years.

1917   February 5: A new constitution is accepted by Carranza's Constitutional Convention, which had convened in December 1916.

1917   May 1: Venustiano Carranza officially becomes the constitutional president, and the Constitution that had been ratified on February 5 comes into effect.

1917   May 18: Montaño is executed for conspiring against Zapata.

1917   June 19: Eufemio Zapata, a day after beating an elderly man to death in a drunken rage, is murdered by the man's son, Sidronio "Loco" Camacho.

1918   At the beginning of the year, Zapata offers Carranza a truce, promising not to continue his opposition to the government if the government leaves Morelos alone.

1918   February: William E. Gates, an American claiming to be a U.S. envoy, visits Zapata in Morelos and tells him that if the various revolutionary factions do not unite to defeat Carranza and make peace, the United States will intervene and impose order on Mexico. After Gates departs, Zapata increases his efforts, which had begun the previous year, to find allies among various revolutionary leaders and forge a unified opposition to Carranza.

1919   April 10: Zapata is gunned down in an ambush.

Chapter 1

A CHILD OF ANENECUILCO, MORELOS

The second son and ninth child of Gabriel Zapata and Cleofas Salazar, Emiliano Zapata Salazar was born on August 8, 1879,[1] in Anenecuilco, a village in the modern state of Morelos that had existed in some form since before 1521, when the Spanish arrived in the region.[2] A cherry-red birthmark in the shape of a hand on his chest is supposed to have immediately revealed his difference from other children,[3] but the significance that is said to have been attributed to the birthmark when Zapata was born is likely a part of his posthumous legend, which also states that he was born during a meteor shower, a sign, according to the village elders, the story goes, that he would be prosperous in life. Another story claims that during his baptism, the baby Zapata swallowed the salt given to him by the priest without crying, something that signified, the priest reportedly said, that he would be an ill-tempered adult.[4] The fact that such legends have been passed down makes determining the difference between the mythical and true stories about Zapata's early life difficult. That his birth was overseen by a *curandera*, an Indian folk healer, and attended by his father as well as his siblings is, however, credible, because that was the custom of the region of his birth, though such details also help to establish the part of the Zapata myth that characterizes his life as a struggle against the advance of modernity, which Zapata had resisted, at least in part, even before he found himself becoming a revolutionary leader.

Zapata's family, although by no means wealthy, was not among the poorest in Anenecuilco. The family lived in an adobe-and-stone home, which measured about 65 square feet, rather than in the simple cane huts that many others in the village would have called home. The Zapatas may also have owned a small plot of land—although their land could very well have been part of the communal property that villagers farmed, the various plots of which were traditionally used by the same families for generations—and they may have rented more land when it was needed from a local hacienda, a Mexican plantation, where Gabriel possibly found employment as some sort of supervisor from time to time. Gabriel, in any case, kept cattle and horses on the land he used, as well as tilled portions of it, and his livelihood, trading his animals and selling such produce as cheese and butter at local markets, allowed the Zapatas to put food—a diet of corn, beans, squash, tortillas, and sometimes turkey, as well as *pozole* stew and chili—on the table every day. This was something many of their neighbors—most of them campesinos (peasants), or *peones* (indentured farm laborers who lived on the haciendas)—struggled to do. Another sign of the Zapatas' relative wealth was that when the family had too much work to handle itself, Gabriel hired some locals to help him complete it. Still, out of the 10 children in the family, only 4—Zapata; his older brother, Eufemio; and 2 of his sisters, Jesucita and Luz[5]—lived into adulthood, something that attests to the hardship endured by even the comparatively well-off residents of Anenecuilco.

The Zapatas, then, were not, as early biographers claimed and the occasional journalist still asserts,[6] campesinos, though they had peasant roots. They were *medieros*,[7] sharecroppers, or, if they did in fact own land, rancheros.[8] As an adult, Zapata would style himself a charro,[9] a Mexican cowboy, partly because of his upbringing and partly because of his pride. But the difference in status between the Zapatas and others in the village, while not unimportant, was less significant than the difference between the hacendados, the owners of the haciendas, and everyone else. The Zapatas, therefore, would become allies of the campesinos when conflicts between villagers and hacendados began to seriously alter the region's social fabric, although Gabriel tended to remain neutral during the early years of Zapata's life, ostensibly accepting the authority wielded by the hacendados, with whom he would have had to remain on good terms if he did in fact rent their land and occasionally work for them.

The threat from the haciendas to the way of life in Morelos, as well as elsewhere in Mexico, became increasingly apparent throughout the 1880s, and it would become obvious to the young Zapata during these years that his, as well as his family's, true sympathy was with the campesinos, despite his father's disinclination to become involved in any opposition. Witnessing the eviction of villagers from the town's last orchard, which was seized by a hacienda when he was about nine, Zapata, according to village lore, said to his teary-eyed father, "When I am a man, *mi padre*, I will put an end to this"[10] and promised that he would win back the land. Although Zapata's part in this story is likely apocryphal, an element of the legend of the revolutionary leader, it does demonstrate the allegiances that those holding the Zapatas' social position would have been expected to have. The story also bears witness to problems that haciendas were creating for the rural populace, and not just in Morelos. A more stark indication of the untenable position campesinos were being asked to accept is illustrated by another, apparently less mythical, story about Zapata's youth. In a neighboring village, residents resisted a hacienda's attempt to appropriate communal land, and the hacendados called in the *rurales*, local troops, and had them burn the village to the ground. Zapata, along with his brother and father, watched the flames from Anenecuilco. That incident had a lasting effect on Zapata, making him become visibly enraged whenever someone reminded him of it throughout the rest of his youth.[11] Closer to home, the two largest haciendas, Cuahuixtla and Hospital, were exerting their freedom to appropriate communally held land in the Mexico of Porfirio Díaz. Cuahuixtla, for example, destroyed homes during a land grab in 1887, while Hospital, in 1895, fenced off pastures and killed the animals grazing on it.

The conflict between the haciendas and the campesinos dated back to the 16th century. In 1529, Hernán Cortés (1485–1547) received from the Spanish king, Charles V, a grant of a territory, the Marquisate of the Valley of Oaxaca, which included the region that became

Morelos. At the same time, municipalities were formed, and the native villages received their communal lands.[12] Cortés's territory was soon afterward divided into haciendas, and by the end of the century, the hacienda system was already in place. The natives' communal lands, as well as the natural resources that the villagers depended on to farm those lands, were, even during this early period, being threatened with appropriation by haciendas, which always seemed to need more land and water for the sugarcane, which the region proved a perfect area for cultivating, that they produced. The exceptions were in such times of economic difficulty as at the end of the 17th century and the beginning of the 19th century, when the demand for sugar decreased. In fact, haciendas almost from the start seemed destined to consume the villages, and, as the historian Samuel Brunk writes, "the very existence of Anenecuilco was . . . endangered [as early as] . . . 1603, when the colonial government suggested that its shrinking population be combined with that of Cuautla," a large town, at least in Zapata's day, to the north of Anenecuilco.[13]

Anenecuilco had survived the early threats it had faced, although other villages were not so lucky, but at the end of the 19th century, the situation became even more troubling. The pace at which haciendas were encroaching upon the traditional system of land distribution dramatically quickened. In Morelos, this quickening was primarily due to the expansion of sugar markets, but an influx of foreign investment in Mexico as a whole and President Díaz's policies, which favored economic expansion through modernization and, therefore, looked favorably on the expansion of haciendas, were also major factors.[14] Consequently, villagers were being forced into peonage, a system in which they would borrow against their future earnings to buy necessities at shops owned by the haciendas on which they lived. Their wages, however, were invariably too small to cover the debts they were amassing, and they were unable to leave the haciendas. They thus, in all practicality, lived as slaves. That system not only helped to modernize Mexico's economy but was also aided by modernization, particularly the expansion of the Mexican railroads between 1877 and 1884. Trains allowed hacendados more easily to bring machinery—specifically, machines developed in the 1870s that could extract more sugar from the cane than was previously possible—to their plantations and sugar to both national and international markets, and the villages in Morelos, which was connected to Mexico City by way of a railway line to Cuautla that was completed in 1881 and extended to Yautepec in 1883, as well as those in other rural regions, were threatened with extinction more so than ever before.[15]

The local hacienda's appropriation of Anenecuilco's last orchard in 1887 or 1888 as well as the *rurales'* burning down of the nearby village, then, were not isolated events but part of a larger trend, one that Zapata would become conscious of as he came of age. He would connect that trend not simply to the forces of modernization—the railway as well as the new machinery—but also to the influence of Spaniards, or at least their Mexican descendents, who seemed always to be associated with innovation. He would, therefore, develop xenophobia, or a hatred of foreigners, and a distrust of culturally European influences on Mexican affairs. These elements of his thinking, as well as the ethnicity of the people whom he defended, encouraged early commentators to identify him as a Tlahuican native, a member of the ethnic group inhabiting the Morelos region prior to the arrival of the Spanish, a mischaracterization that is carried on in a lesser form by Peter E. Newell when he calls Zapata "almost pure Tlahuican."[16] The Zapatas, however, were mestizos, that is, they were of Spanish and native descent, and their Spanish ancestors can be traced back to the earliest European settlers, to one of the men who rode with Cortés during his conquest of the region, in fact. Still, Zapata's face, as the biographer Roger Parkinson notes, "revealed Indian ancestry: swarthy, high cheekbones, dark eyes, thick black hair."[17] Thus Zapata's own identification of himself as a member of the native people, something evinced by his xenophobia if nothing else, would never have seemed a simple affectation on his part.

A sense of social, class, or racial affiliation was not the only thing that encouraged Zapata to identify or align himself with campesinos. He would have shared common experiences with their children while he was growing up. Some aspects of his upbringing no doubt differed from poorer children in his village. Zapata, for example, had access to horses from an early age, which many of his peers would not have had. Another story of his youth tells of his taking his Aunt Crispina's horse and riding it bareback as fast as he could through nearby underbrush.

Unfazed by the danger he had placed himself in, he merely bragged about his ability to hang on to the animal when he returned a few moments later.[18] He was also provided with a basic education, as his father, "to get him out of the sun, and so he can learn a little,"[19] sent Zapata to a school in nearby Villa de Ayala, when he was around seven. There, he learned to read and write and may have also learned basic Mexican history and bookkeeping,[20] but his education would have always been subordinate to the work that needed to get done at home or in the fields.

That work, which would have been considered more important to learn to do for the future Zapata was expected to have, included planting and harvesting, burning lime in the local hills, hauling feed to the animals and wood for fires to his house, tending livestock, churning butter, as well as doing household chores for his aunt, who was a close neighbor. In fact, even as he began school, his father set about preparing him for adult responsibilities, giving him a mule for which to care. He would get other animals of his own as he grew older and proved himself capable of tending to them, including a mare named La Papaya from his father; a cow from his maternal grandmother, Doña Vicenta Cerezo de Salazar; and cows, mules, and horses from those in the village for whom he did occasional work.[21] His attendance at school would have suffered as a result of his growing responsibilities at home, and as soon as he was old enough to be more useful to his family, a couple of years after he had begun his education, Zapata was taken out of school altogether. From then on, he labored as hard, at least at times, as any campesino, sharing with them the rhythm of the days and seasons.

Like others in the village, Zapata would come to look forward to Sundays and the annual week-long fiesta, or festival, at Cuautla, as well as saint's days, the times when markets were held. During the Cuautla fiesta, people from numerous villages would converge on the town to trade their products, each village traditionally bringing particular commodities. (Those from Cuernavaca sold pottery; from Jonacatepec, limes; from Yautepec, oranges; from Cuautla, leather goods; and from Iguala, silver jewelry.) These gatherings had more than economic importance: they also helped to break up the monotony of the people's daily routines. Zapata was able to don clothes more extravagant than the sandals and the white shirts and pants that he would likely have worn in the fields and around his home day in and day out. During his teens, his style earned him a reputation for being a dandy. He is known, for example, to have worn trousers covered in silver coins that were given to him by his uncle Cristino, though his more usual look involved dressing up, as Newell writes, "*charro*-style, all in black, or in a short leather jacket embroidered with gold thread, with tight fitting trousers complete with silver trimming down the seams, and an enormous silver-laden sombrero."[22]

Such a dandyish look was, in most contexts, likely to be scoffed at by boys and men alike in small Mexican villages, where machismo was important, but Zapata reportedly did not suffer any ridicule. Perhaps he escaped scorn because his clothes "formed a uniform," as Parkinson notes in a discussion of the outfits Zapata wore when he first displayed his forces in April 1911. Parkinson goes on to remark, "Zapata dressed as a typical village chief wearing his best clothes for the local fair."[23] Thus his early use of such dress may have been accepted as a sign of the significance of his family in the 19th-century history of Anenecuilco in which members of both his mother's and father's family had taken roles, sometimes significant ones. Indeed, the coin-covered pants that Zapata owned were made to commemorate his uncle Cristino's part in a campaign against bandits known as the *plateados*, or "men dressed in silver."[24] Zapata's other uncle, José, or Chema, the nickname by which he went, gave Zapata a muzzle-loading rifle from the same campaign.

Zapata's growing status as a promising horseman, which he began to make a name for himself as a teenager at rodeos on market days and during the fiestas, also may have contributed to his ability to appear a dandy without being mocked. Zapata had begun learning to perform jumps on his horse—a skill that his father, also a good horseman, knew would be important for him to master—by the time he was 12. As soon as he became good enough, after rough training that involved scolding rather than comfort when he fell, which reportedly made the young Zapata more determined, Zapata began displaying his skills at regional rodeos. Horse jumping was not the only talent that he brought to such events. He also proved successful riding bucking bulls and capturing and wrangling running steers to the ground. Zapata, legend has it, became the star of the local rodeos and is believed to have earned, as

Carlos M. Jiménez writes, "the reputation of being the finest horseman in the state of Morelos."[25]

Another skill Zapata had to learn growing up was the use of firearms. Guns were almost as much a part of his life as horses throughout his childhood, and he was taught to handle them by his father's brothers, Cristino and José, the latter of which took the young Emiliano deer hunting. These uncles also told Zapata stories about his family's part in Anenecuilco's, as well as Mexico's, history, helping to shape the consciousness that would lead Emiliano to take the part he took in his nation's history. The stories of both his maternal and paternal family demonstrated to him the importance, and perhaps the value, of fighting for the good of Mexico. Zapata's maternal grandfather, José Salazar, had been involved in the early 19th-century conflict against the Spanish in which Mexico won its independence, smuggling, while still a child, supplies to Mexican insurgents who were trapped at Cuautla. Cristino and José had fought against the French Intervention in the 1860s,[26] and Zapata's great uncle, also José, had been a leader of local forces during the same conflict and had become the village's chief elder in 1867, a post he kept until his death in 1876.

Around 1896, both Zapata's parents died within a year of one another, leaving Eufemio, then in his early to mid-20s, in charge of the family. Jesucita had already married and was living with her husband, while Luz remained for a while in the family home, though she soon married and left, too. Eufemio, known for being something of a rough character and hard drinker, as well as a womanizer, would depart sometime afterwards, selling his portion of the family's land or the rights to work his portion of the communal property, if the family did not in fact own it.[27] He first went to Veracruz to become a peddler and then to Orizba, where he was a fruit merchant, though he would return to Anenecuilco from Veracruz, where he had again taken up residence, when the revolution broke out. Zapata stayed behind, having developed deep affection for his home and the life that it had to offer him. To establish his financial independence, he bought mules with which he hauled corn to markets for local farmers, as well as bricks and lime for construction projects to the Chinameca hacienda. He also continued farming, particularly watermelon. Proud of his entrepreneurial skills, he once noted, "One of the happiest days of my life was when

I made around five or six hundred pesos from a crop of watermelons I raised all on my own."[28] If Mexico had remained peaceful, Zapata would likely have lived out his days as a local entrepreneur, working on his land and with animals, both his own and others, or, to put it more strikingly, he would have been a successful version of his grandson, also named Emiliano Zapata, who, although not a legitimate heir, came to live in his grandfather's ancestral home, eking out a poor living selling pork and working for others, sometimes on sugar haciendas.[29]

NOTES

1. Zapata's date of birth, the one recent biographers invariably use, is given by tradition. Zapata, however, may have been born, as Samuel Brunk's research reveals, on July 20. August 8, the feast day of the saint after whom he was named, may be the day he was baptized. (See Brunk's *Emiliano Zapata! Revolution and Betrayal in Mexico* [Albuquerque: University of New Mexico Press, 1995], 245n8.) Brunk, nonetheless, gives August 8 within his text. Uncertainty over the year also exists; the possibilities range from 1873 to 1883. (See John Womack, *Zapata and the Mexican Revolution* [New York: Vintage Books, 1970 (1968)], 5n5. Womack himself gives the year as 1879.)

2. Morelos, which lies just to the south of Mexico City, was founded in 1869. See John H. McNeely, "Origins of the Zapata Revolt in Morelos," *Hispanic American Historical Review* 46, no. 2 (May 1966), 153–69.

3. As Jesse Katz notes "in the folklore of the Mexican Revolution, Zapata's birth is said to have been foretold by a local witch doctor, the infant's destiny confirmed by a birthmark, on his chest, in the shape of a tiny hand." See "The Curse of Zapata," *Los Angeles Magazine* 47 (December 1, 2002), 176.

4. Samuel Brunk, *The Posthumous Career of Emiliano Zapata* (Austin: University of Texas Press, 2008), 57.

5. The surviving sisters' proper names were María de Jesús and María de Luz (see Frank McLynn, *Villa and Zapata: A History of the Mexican Revolution* [New York: Carroll & Graf, 2002], 41). Some sources conjecture that a fifth child may have grown into adulthood (see, for example, Brunk, *Emiliano Zapata!*, 6).

6. See, for example, Katz, "Curse of Zapata," 103.

7. See Roger Parkinson, *Zapata: A Biography* (Briarcliff Manor, NY: Stein & Day, 1980 [1975]), 21.

8. Peter E. Newell, *Zapata of Mexico* (Montreal: Black Rose Books, 1997), 14.

9. Mario T. García notes that the difference between a campesino and a charro is not simply a class difference but a cultural one as well. See *Luis Leal: An Auto/Biography* (Austin: University of Texas Press, 2000), 183.

10. Quoted in Newell, *Zapata of Mexico*, 16.

11. See McLynn, *Villa and Zapata*, 38–39.

12. See McNeely, "Origins of the Zapata Revolt in Morelos," 154.

13. Brunk, *Emiliano Zapata!*, 10.

14. Without the support of the government, after all, hacendados could have been stopped from appropriating land through legal means.

15. See Womack, *Zapata and the Mexican Revolution*, 15.

16. Newell, *Zapata of Mexico*, 14; See also Rosa E. King, *Tempest over Mexico: A Personal Chronicle* (New York: Little Brown, 1940 [1935]); Irving Werstein, *Land and Liberty* (New York: Cowles, 1971); and MacKinley Helm, *Mexican Painters: Rivera, Orozco, Siqueiros and Other Artists of the Social Realist School* (Mineola, NY: Courier Dover, 1989 [1941]). King refers to Zapata as "an almost unknown Indian" (77); Werstein calls him "a pure-blooded Mexican" (53); and Helm describes him as "the Indian bushmaster" (15).

17. Parkinson, *Zapata: A Biography*, 19.

18. Brunk, *Emiliano Zapata!*, 7.

19. Quoted in Brunk, *Emiliano Zapata!*, 6.

20. Brunk, in *Emiliano Zapata!*, conjectures that Mexican history would have been introduced to the young students (6), whereas McLynn, in *Villa and Zapata*, asserts that bookkeeping would have been taught, perhaps to prepare students for their business dealings later in life (39).

21. Lola E. Boyd, "Zapata," *Américas* 20, no. 9 (September 1968), 2.

22. Newell, *Zapata of Mexico*, 17.

23. Parkinson, *Zapata: A Biography*, 59. Parkinson also observes that Zapata's reputation for being a dandy outside Mexico is "largely false,"

the product of outsiders' misunderstanding the nature of the village chief's uniform; the bit of truth to the notion that Parkinson acknowledges with the qualifier "largely" likely relates to Zapata's widely reported preference for extravagant clothing early in his life.

24. McLynn, *Villa and Zapata*, 38. See also Enrique Krauze's *Mexico: Biography of Power; A History of Modern Mexico, 1810–1996*, trans. Hank Heifetz (New York: HarperCollins, 1998), 278.

25. Carlos M. Jiménez, *The Mexican American Heritage*, 2nd ed. (Austin: University of Texas Press, 1994), 126.

26. Napoleon III of France, with the support of England and Spain, invaded Mexico in 1862. England and Spain withdrew their support once Napoleon's intention to aid conservatives in setting up a monarchy in Mexico became clear. France forged ahead, nonetheless, making, in 1864, the Austrian Archduke Maximilian the emperor of Mexico, an inept ruler whose government collapsed in 1867. For a fuller account of this conflict, see Joan Haslip's *The Crown of Mexico: Maximilian and his Empress Carlota* (New York: Holt, Rinehart and Winston, 1972).

27. Werstein, in *Land and Liberty*, relates an alternative story, which asserts that "Eufemio took his share of the money [that he and Zapata saved from their watermelon business] and went off to Veracruz" (54). Most historians, even those who are skeptical of the assertions that the Zapatas owned their own land, believe Eufemio raised the money he needed to leave Anenecuilco from selling land.

28. Krauze, *Mexico: Biography of Power*, 279.

29. For discussions of the life of Zapata's grandson, see Alvaro Vargas Llosa, "History of the Mexican Revolution Shows Why Migration Continues Today," *Deseret Morning News* (November 7, 2007), http://www.lexis-nexis.com/ and Hayes Ferguson, "Zapata Symbolizes Failure: Much of Mexico Still in Poverty," *Times-Picayune* (July 8, 1998), A1, http://www.lexis-nexis.com/.

Chapter 2

ZAPATA'S EARLY POLITICAL EDUCATION

In June 1897—which was the year that Zapata would date the beginning of his serious opposition to Díaz's political regime—Zapata found himself in enough trouble to warrant his being arrested. Having conflicts with the authorities was nothing strange for young men, especially those who were members of Zapata's class, in Mexican villages, and the exact nature of his crime is not known for certain. A variety of accounts have been published, many of them asserting that Zapata's transgression involved early attempts to resist the haciendas on a local level, including one that states that he had taken to the roads with his brother to dole out justice to those taking campesinos' lands away or those who were supporting those who did, and another that claims he took part in a protest against a hacienda that had recently appropriated lands.[1] The most credible story asserts that Zapata, arguing about the land issue with a more affluent member of the community at a local fiesta, got into a fight, and having earned a reputation as a potential subversive, he was taken into custody by the local police. Before Zapata could be brought to jail, however, Eufemio, who either had not yet left Anenecuilco or had returned for the fiesta, intervened with the help of a group of friends. Eufemio reportedly drew his gun and demanded that the arresting officers set Emiliano free. The officers complied, and the two Zapatas escaped, taking refuge in the nearby state of Puebla, where Emiliano got a job on the Jaltepec hacienda with the help of family friends.

Zapata remained in Jaltepec for about year, working with animals, perhaps with horses in the stables, and returned home after his family and friends were able to secure his safety in Anenecuilco. Little is known about his life for the next few years, though he seems to have continued to come into conflict with local authorities. Those in Anenecuilco later recalled, "'Miliano was a brave man who would not take any crap; as a result, already during the time of peace, he was often in trouble."[2] He certainly must have continued to pursue his entrepreneurial activities, farming, sometimes on the property of a local hacienda, the owner of which would have received half of the profits that Zapata would earn from that land; hauling commodities on his mules; and probably beginning to train horses, a skill for which he would earn a reputation during the first decade of the 20th century. In any event, he acquired at some point his own land and a stable, things he owned in 1911.[3]

The first opposition to the hacendados' activities in which Zapata may have been seriously involved concerned a dispute between Yautepec, a nearby village where relatives of his mother lived, and Pablo Escandón's Atlihuayán hacienda. In 1904, Zapata reportedly joined a Yautepec delegation of no less than 60, although it may have had as many as 75, members[4] that met with President Díaz. Led by Jovito Serrano, the man whom Yautepec's villagers had chosen to serve as their leader, the delegation discussed with Díaz a problem that had begun in either 1902 or 1903.[5] Escandón ordered those working at his hacienda to fence off 3,500 acres of communal property. The cattle that had been grazing on the land broke back into it, and the hacienda kept them—at least those that did not die from neglect or that were not sold—until the villagers paid a hefty fine. Not only that, they also had some of the cattle's owners arrested. The fine may have been unjust, but it was a small price in comparison to the loss of the village land. Yautepec, therefore, sought redress through legal means, bringing its case to the local courts, which ruled in Escandón's favor. The villagers pressed on, filing an appeal with Cuernavaca's district court, which upheld the lower court's decision and also imposed another fine on the villagers. Finally, the village brought its case to Mexico's Supreme Court.

Francisco Serralde, a lawyer who had a history of taking cases that contested the status quo, was assisting Serrano as the Supreme Court hearing neared and seems to have had a hand in getting Díaz to meet with the Yautepec delegation. Having seen the danger that such cases represented for Mexico, Serralde wrote to Díaz, warning him: "If the Supreme Court does not give these men justice, you may be sure . . . that there will soon be a revolution."[6] Díaz did not regard the matter with the import that Serralde attributed to it. Díaz, after all, had ruled Mexico unopposed since 1876. He was not, it is true, officially the president from 1880 to 1884, having changed the constitution in 1876 to bar the president from running for office a second time, but the period during which Díaz was out of office, his minister of war and friend General Manuel González served as president, having won the office in an election that was manipulated by Díaz. At the end of González's term, Díaz arranged to have the constitution changed again, allowing him to become president for another term. Six years later, he pushed through a constitutional amendment that allowed him to remain president for life. Díaz, therefore, could hardly have believed that a small group of peasants was capable of starting a significant revolution.

Whatever the reason Díaz had for agreeing to meet with the delegation, helping Yautepec's search for justice was the last thing on his mind: he supported the hacendados and was a friend of Escandón. Still, while he listened to the villagers, he expressed sympathy and offered his support by giving Serrano the name of another lawyer to whom he could go for help. In June 1904, the Supreme Court ruled in favor of the hacienda. Serrano was soon arrested and the documents proving that the fenced-off land legally belonged to the village, which he had hoped would lead the case to be settled in Yautepec's favor, were seized. Serrano was sent to a labor camp in Quintana Roo, where he died from overwork and illness in November 1905.[7] Zapata's involvement in this conflict, if he was involved at all, would have been minor, though early accounts asserted that Zapata angrily confronted Díaz, a story that is certainly an invention, as Zapata avoided arrest. He would have been more likely to observe quietly, as he was taciturn by nature, and learn all he could. The confrontation between Yautepec and the legal system, whatever his involvement was in it, would have contributed to Zapata's political education. If he were among those who met Díaz, he would have certainly been involved in some capacity in the village's struggle for justice prior to the delegation's travelling to Mexico City. If he had not been a member of the delegation, he would have listened to local discussions of the matter and grasped the relevant lesson.

Zapata, in any case, soon began his education in a more personal setting. Yautepec's experience or perhaps the commonness of land grabs in Morelos led those in Anenecuilco to see the need to begin seeking legal means to protect its communal interests against the encroachment of haciendas. They began their own search for the titles of their communal land in 1904, particularly lands that the hacienda Hospital had appropriated, despite such evidence proving futile in Yautepec's case. Zapata's involvement in this endeavor is more certain, though the exact role that he took in it isn't known. What is known is that in 1906, Anenecuilco's activities become serious enough to get the attention of Morelos's governor, Manuel Alarcón, a hacienda owner himself. In that year, Alarcón brought representatives from the hacienda Hospital and the village of Anenecuilco, as well as Villa de Ayala, together to discuss the matter under the direction of the *jefe político*, that is, the political leader, of Cuautla. Zapata's involvement is shown by his taking part in this meeting, though nothing was resolved at it. The following year, Anenecuilco's representatives attempted, but failed, to discuss the matter with Díaz, who was in Morelos in February 1907 for health reasons. A few months later, Anenecuilco submitted its titles to Alarcón in the hope of finally settling the issue, although he had yet to do anything by the time he died on December 15, 1908.

During this period, Zapata continued his business activities, which had apparently grown large enough that he sometimes, as his father had done, hired locals to help complete the amount of work that needed to get done. Zapata also expanded the scope of his political education. Searching for land titles and attempting to use them to thwart the haciendas with the help of the courts and politicians provided practical experience, illustrating the unhelpful, as well as corrupt, nature of the system, but the arrival of two men in the area led Zapata to dabble in more intellectual pursuits—although he would never really aspire to the status of an intellectual. The first of these men was Pablo Torres

Burgos, a former schoolteacher who would come to eke out a living as a shopkeeper and who also became a legal advisor to small farmers in the area. In 1906, he came to Anenecuilco, though he would take up residence in Villa de Ayala by 1909. He befriended Zapata, sharing with him such reading materials as the anti-Díaz papers *El Diario del Hogar*, a liberal publication, and *Regeneración*, an anarchist publication. Torres Burgos guidance was soon aided by Otilio Montaño, who had grown up with Zapata in Anenecuilco but, unenthusiastic about the idea of becoming a farm laborer, had acquired enough of an education to have become a schoolteacher. He had taught in a number of schools in Morelos, but sometime in 1906, he came back in Anenecuilco and began actively propagating his anti-government views, giving public lectures that Zapata attended. He introduced Zapata to the thought and work of Peter Kropotkin, a 19th-century Russian prince who became an anarchist intellectual, opposing the idea of a central government in favor of independent communities of workers,[8] an idea that Zapata may have come to see as similar to the traditional Mexican village system.

Montaño made a greater impression on Zapata than Torres Burgos, perhaps because Zapata was impressed by Montaño's enthusiasm. Montaño's status as an educated local may also have played a role, as it would have garnered the respect of many in the area. In any case, Montaño became Zapata's *campadre*—"the highest tribute one friend could pay another"[9]—and the godfather of his first son, Nicolás, who was born to Inés Aguilar in 1906,[10] the year Zapata is said to have begun cohabiting with her, perhaps in Cuautla, though if their home were there, the arrangement certainly wasn't fulltime. She would have Zapata's daughter, or perhaps two of his daughters, before 1910, the year Zapata left her. By that point, he had been courting Josefa Espejo, whose father was a prosperous livestock dealer in Villa de Ayala until his death in 1909 and whom Zapata would marry legitimately in 1911. His relationship with Josefa was almost certainly more chaste than the one he had had with other women, as he sought her as a wife. His initial proposal to her, made in 1909 or before, may have been rejected because her father did not regard him as a suitable husband because of his social status. Zapata, in any case, had always had success with women, apparently due to his romantic charm rather than rough handling—an approach to courtship that his brother is remembered to have favored. He was likely not faithful to Inés during the years they lived together and was certainly not faithful to Josefa during their marriage. Indeed, he had between five and seven illegitimate children, though the number could be higher, many of whom were born after 1911,[11] and of the children he had, those who would defend his legacy would be the illegitimate ones, for Josefa's two children died before reaching adulthood. The most prominent of these were Nicolás, Ana María, Diego, and Mateo, all of whom became involved in Mexico's politics; the latter three were even actively using their name, or their father's, to throw support behind particular political parties at the beginning of this century.[12] Ana María was perhaps the most successful, becoming the head of the Union of Morelos Women in her teens, and after fighting for women's political rights in the name of her father for two decades, "she became the first female congressional deputy from Morelos."[13]

Throughout the years of his involvement with Aguilar, Zapata earned more and more of a name for himself with the authorities, and in 1908 he was again forced to flee Morelos, almost certainly because of the role he was taking in Anenecuilco's fight against local haciendas. He again found work in Puebla, training horses on an estate near Chietla.[14] Zapata's second period of exile was short. He was back home by the end of the year or early in 1909, when he became active in a movement to elect a governor other than the one Díaz had preapproved. The election was significant because of the fact that an opposition candidate actually played a role it. For more than thirty years, Díaz had not allowed opposition parties to form, and during every election, the winners, all of them supporters of Díaz and his policies, were determined before anyone had cast a ballot. The idea of putting forth a candidate to challenge the one Díaz had picked at this point was prompted by remarks he had made. In an interview that Díaz had given to the American journalist James Creelman that was published in the March 1908 issue of *Pearson's Magazine* and was translated for Mexican readers and published in the pro-Díaz *El Imparcial* around the same time, Díaz had not only asserted that he was retiring from politics "when my present term of office ends" in 1910 but also said that he welcomed "an opposition party. . . . If it appears, I will regard it as a blessing, not an evil. And if it can develop power . . . I will stand by it, advise it and forget myself in the successful inauguration of complete democratic government."[15]

Díaz was posturing for Creelman, as he had done for others on previous occasions, but this time the words had greater significance, leaving those who would oppose him wondering about what their next move should be. As the historian John Womack puts it, "Díaz was getting old and could not hide it. Before, talk about retiring was only breath wasted and forgotten. Now, in 1908, it was a morbid reminder that whether he retired or not, he would soon die, and then times would change."[16] Almost a year passed before anyone would attempt to take Díaz at his word, even though a number of elections, six gubernatorial races as well as congressional ones on both state and federal levels, had taken place. Alarcón, whose savvy in handling campesinos without taking anything away from hacendados had made him a valuable asset for the Díaz regime in Morelos, was among those who were elected in 1908. His death sparked the first experiment in which people organized in an attempt to take Díaz at his word.

The problem wasn't exactly that Alarcón was gone; others, perhaps as savvy as he was, could have been chosen to succeed him. But at the urging of prominent men in Morelos, Díaz agreed to appoint Escandón, a man whom the hacendados thought would allow them to do as they pleased without attempting to suggest to campesinos that they had any rights. Those concerned about the situation of the villages immediately set out to find a candidate to oppose Escandón. The perfect man, they thought, would be General Francisco Leyva, who had been a hero during the French Intervention, had governed the state before Díaz came to power, and had retained widespread respect in it, even though he was living in Mexico City. Representatives from the state travelled to Mexico City to propose to Leyva the idea of his running for office. Feeling his age made him unfit to reenter politics, the general decided against becoming a candidate. Instead, he suggested that one of his sons could take his place. Patricio Leyva was then chosen, and after some hesitation, a result of the organizers' concerns over how Díaz would react, the Leyvistas held a convention on January 7, 1909, in Cuernavaca, Morelos's capital, and officially nominated Patricio. The election would be held a month later on February 7.

Zapata would not have been involved in the politicking that was taking place in Cuernavaca. He was far from the center of action. He soon took an interest in the hope that an opposition candidate might offer, however, especially after the direction of the Leyvista movement shifted its focus. The *Leyvistas* were not initially out to win the election, despite their putting forth a candidate. Rather, they wanted to discuss, and actually began to do so, the problem of Escandón's candidacy with Díaz's political machine so that a more acceptable candidate could be found. That plan, while never completely abandoned, was altered when an independent group from Mexico City, the Democrats, became involved and started working toward getting Leyva votes. They began establishing political clubs throughout Morelos, about 25 in all, in the latter part of January. One of these clubs, Melchor Ocampo, was formed in Villa de Ayala under the leadership of Torres Burgos and two other local figures, Refugio Yáñez and Luciano Cabrera.[17] On January 24, Zapata officially joined this club. Shortly thereafter, he signed, along with other *Leyvistas*, a letter protesting the electoral fraud that was expected, a letter that was printed by the national press, which was following the Morelos election closely. Beyond these small gestures, Zapata is not known to have done much else.

The seditious nature of the events surrounding electing Morelos's governor escalated, illustrating the volatility of the rural populous. Two days before Zapata joined the Villa de Ayala Leyvista club, 1,500 people rallied in Cuautla to celebrate the formation of such a club in that town. That was on a Friday, and two days later, the club hoped to stage a rally that could be attended by those who had had to work during the first one. The town's *jefe político*, Enrique Dabbadie, refused permission. Indeed, as Womack writes, "he had practically put the town under martial law, with federal troops and police and municipal gendarmes everywhere,"[18] and ordered them to break up demonstrations.[19] During the following week, at Leyvista campaign rallies in Anenecuilco and Villa de Ayala, crowds yelled "'*muchos vivas*' for Leyva and shouted out '*algunos mueras* [death to] *al* Señor Escandón.'"[20] The lieutenant governor, Luis Flores, who had been reporting on the situation to Díaz, had suspected agitators arrested. Despite the threat of arrest, villagers attended such rallies across Morelos. Speakers, to animated applause, began to promise that Leyva would, if elected, return land and water rights that had been stolen for the use of haciendas, though such promises were denied having been made when election day got closer and the subversive nature of them seemed to encourage trouble. More astute or perhaps less arrogant observers might have seen larger problems for the Díaz regime than an embarrassing election, but those in power only saw troublemakers who needed to be suppressed so that Díaz's candidate could become governor.

In the meantime, permission had been granted to hold a Leyvista rally in Cuautla on Sunday, January 31. When the day arrived, the period in which it was allowed to be held was limited to two hours, and *rurales* lined the streets, keeping an eye on the situation. There were few problems, although the people's enthusiasm for the pro-village perspective that speakers articulated disturbed authorities. The next day, during an Escandón rally, also in Cuautla, the situation seemed more troubling. As professional speakers, who had been brought down from Mexico City, gave speeches in support of Escandón, cheers for Leyva were occasionally shouted, as well as threatening comments. One of the speakers, Hipólito Olea, shouted back when his speech was met with rallying cries for Leyva, berating the people for being stupid and ungrateful. The crowd responded by throwing rocks, and as the *rurales* readied themselves to fire, the people scattered. After the scene calmed down, Dabbadie had Burgos Torres and others arrested, even though the people who had started the trouble couldn't be identified. The arrests continued throughout the week, turning Cuautla into the area in which the most Leyvista supporters were jailed.

Despite widespread support for Leyva, Escandón went on to win the election with the help of a number of underhanded precautions taken by the *jefe políticos*, including arresting Leyva supporters, refusing to allow those who were suspected of favoring Leyva to vote, and stuffing ballot boxes. Escandón was sworn into office on March 15, partially against his better judgment. He would later tell his friend Rosa King, "I didn't want to be governor. I told Porfirito I didn't want the appointment. Why do I have to mix in these beastly local politics?"[21] Escandón would do as little mixing as possible, staying out of Morelos as much as he could possibly get away with as the governor and allowing local *jefe políticos* to do as they pleased, which often left the campesinos and *peones*, as well as better off villagers, at the mercy of small tyrants. Villagers' struggle to keep their communal land now became more difficult, for Escandón almost inevitably settled any disputes that came before him in favor of the haciendas. He also openly displayed his indifference to village rights through decrees, legislation, and constitutional reforms on the state level that were enacted to strip villagers of their rights and perhaps served to relieve him of the burden of becoming personally involved in disputes.

The more difficult situation in Morelos led Anenecuilco's village elders to resign from their posts about six months after Escandón became governor. Deciding that younger, more energetic leaders were needed, they called a meeting on September 12, 1909, to announce their resolution and hold elections for the new office holders. José Merino, Zapata's uncle, resigned from his position as village council president, giving a short speech in which he may have implied the changes in Morelos might force villagers to take up guns to protect themselves. Zapata was among the three people nominated to replace Merino; the other two were Modesto González and Bartolo Parral, whom Zapata nominated and who nominated Zapata in turn. Zapata was elected by a clear majority, partly, historians suppose, because of the importance his family had in Anenecuilco's history, partly because of his modest financial success, and partly because of his reputation for standing up to authority. Zapata did not immediately alter the course that had been followed for years to protect the town's communal lands. He continued to pursue the legal methods that his predecessor had employed, relying on titles and hiring a lawyer, whom he traveled to Mexico City to find on September 27, to fight cases before the court.

As it had in the past, the legal system proved itself unwilling to aid the villagers, and things seemed much worse the following spring. Zapata himself was not in Anenecuilco at that time. At the beginning of 1910, when he ended his relationship with Aguilar, either her father or her uncle—Remigio Alfaro—filed a complaint against him. That complaint, coupled with a charge of public drunkenness, was enough to get Zapata conscripted into the army, though his growing reputation as one fighting against the Porfirian machine probably also contributed to the sentence—a stint in the army would get him out of the way. In any case, Zapata was placed in a regiment in Cuernavaca on February 11, where he was, according to some sources, almost immediately promoted to the rank of sergeant. The following month, he had been discharged from the service with the help, it seems, of Ignacio de la Torre y Mier, Díaz's son-in-law and Morelos's federal deputy. In exchange for his freedom, Zapata was obliged to work in Ignacio's stables as chief groom in Mexico City. Holding that position only served to inflame his resentment of the Porfirian regime, for Ignacio's horses lived in greater luxury than campesinos back in Anenecuilco, where the situation was becoming dire.

Beginning in March, the Hospital hacienda stopped the villagers from farming land they had used for generations, sending men with weapons to stand by the fields just as the planting season was arriving. A month went by and the hacienda continued to prevent any farming. The village council wrote to the governor, pleading for relief and practically admitting that the village understood that it would lose its rights to the land.

> As the rainy season is about to begin, we poor workingmen must begin getting the land ready for planting. For this reason . . . we turn to the Superior Government of the state, imploring its protection so that, if it please, it might concede to us its backing so we can plant the fields without fear of being plundered and run off by the proprietors of Hospital hacienda. We are disposed to recognize whoever turns out to be the owner of the fields, be it the village of San Miguel Anenecuilco or someone else. But we want to plant the fields so as not to be ruined, because farming is what gives us life. From it we get sustenance and that of our families.[22]

Escandón's office wrote back a little more than a week later, asking for more specifics about the land under question. The council quickly sent the required information, only to be told that the hacienda had been informed of the notes and would do what it thought was for the best. The hacienda manager made his boss's intentions known, remarking, "If that rabble from Anenecuilco wants to farm, let them farm in a flower-pot, because they're not getting any land, even up the side of the hills."[23] Just as the rains began to fall, the hacienda rented the land to farmers from Villa de Ayala, who began planting. Those in Anenecuilco looked on, believing they could do nothing.

NOTES

1. See David W. Del Testa, "Zapata, Emiliano: Mexican Revolutionary, 1879–1919," in *Government Leaders, Military Rulers, and Political Activists*, ed. David W. Del Testa et al. (Westport, CT: Greenwood, 2001), 202; and Samuel Brunk, *Emiliano Zapata! Revolution and Betrayal in Mexico* (Albuquerque: University of New Mexico Press, 1995), 14–15.

2. Quoted in Brunk, *Emiliano Zapata!*, 15.

3. "I've got some land and a stable . . . which I earned through long years of honest work and not through political campaigns," Zapata told a reporter in 1911. Quoted in John Womack, *Zapata and the Mexican Revolution* (New York: Vintage Books, 1970 [1968]), 128.

4. See John H. McNeely, "Origins of the Zapata Revolt in Morelos," *Hispanic American Historical Review* 46, no. 2 (May 1966), 155. Womack claims there were 70 (*Zapata and the Mexican Revolution*, 50), while Peter E. Newell writes 75 (see *Zapata of Mexico* [Montreal: Black Rose Books, 1997], 13).

5. The conflict took place between 1902 and 1905. Newell dates its beginning in 1903 (*Zapata of Mexico*, 13). The Supreme Court made its ruling in June 1904, so the meeting with Díaz must have been earlier than that. For the date of the Supreme Court ruling, see Womack, *Zapata and the Mexican Revolution*, 51 and Stanton Arthur Coblentz, *The Militant Dissenters* (London: A. S. Barnes, 1970), 123.

6. Quoted in Enrique Krauze, *Mexico: Biography of Power; A History of Modern Mexico, 1810–1996*, trans. Hank Heifetz (New York: Harper Collins, 1998), 280.

7. See Womack, *Zapata and the Mexican Revolution*, 50–51 and Brunk, *Emiliano Zapata!*, 16.

8. See, for example, Peter Kropotkin, *Evolution and Environment*, ed. George Woodcock (Montreal: Black Rose Books, 1996).

9. Frank McLynn, *Villa and Zapata: A History of the Mexican Revolution* (New York: Carroll & Graf, 2002), 43.

10. Some sources date the beginning of Zapata's cohabitation with Aguilar in 1908 and assert that he had kidnapped her and that her father had him arrested and forced into the army as a result. Those versions lack an air of credibility, failing to account for Zapata's ability to father two or three children with Aguilar in the short amount of time that he would have been with her in 1908 before being forced into the army that same year. (See Krauze, *Mexico: Biography of Power*, 280 and McLynn, *Villa and Zapata*, 47 for variations of this version of the story.) Brunk, *Emiliano Zapata!*, 25–26 gives the 1906–1910 dates.

11. Roger Parkinson, *Zapata: A Biography* (Briarcliff Manor, NY: Stein & Day, 1980 [1975]), 14, says "perhaps as many as five," while William Weber Johnson, in a review of John Womack's *Zapata and the Mexican Revolution*, puts the number at "at least seven" (see "Zapata: A Conservative Old Red," *Life* 66, no. 7 [February 21, 1969], 16); McLynn claims that Zapata, besides the children he had with Aguilar and with his wife, had "three other children with other women, born in 1913–14: Eugenio, María Elena and Ana María" (*Villa and Zapata*, 284). Brunk mentions another daughter, Paulina, in passing (see *Emiliano Zapata!*, 225). Two other sons, Diego and Mateo, were also recognized by Zapata as his own. See "Obits for Bernard Coutaz, Barry Hannah, A[na María] Zapata Portillo," *Washington Post* (March 4, 2010), http://www.washingtonpost.com/wp-dyn/content/article/2010/03/03/AR2010030303851.html, which gives Ana María's year of birth as 1915.

12. See Samuel Brunk, "The Mortal Remains of Emiliano Zapata," in *Death, Dismemberment, and Memory: Body Politics in Latin America*, ed. Lyman L. Johnson (Albuquerque: University of New Mexico Press, 2004), 143.

13. Samuel Brunk, *The Posthumous Career of Emiliano Zapata* (Austin: University of Texas Press, 2008), 143. For Ana María's affiliation with the Union of Morelos Women, see pages 115 and 128.

14. Brunk (see *Emiliano Zapata!*, 16) believes that Zapata went to Chietla; others note that he was out of Morelos for some time at the end of 1908 and possibly the beginning of 1909 but believe that he was in the army at this time because of the trouble he had with Inés Aquilar's family.

15. Quoted in James Creelman, "President Díaz: Hero of the Americas," *Pearson's Magazine* (March 1908), 242.

16. Womack, *Zapata and the Mexican Revolution*, 11.

17. Ibid., 24–28.

18. Ibid., 32.

19. See Alan Knight, *The Mexican Revolution*, vol. 2 (Lincoln: University of Nebraska Press, 1990), 25–26.

20. Quoted in Paul Hart, *Bitter Harvest* (Albuquerque: University of New Mexico Press, 2005), 189.

21. Rosa E. King, *Tempest over Mexico: A Personal Chronicle* (New York: Little Brown, 1940 [1935]), 35.

22. Quoted in Womack, *Zapata and the Mexican Revolution*, 52.

23. Quoted in Parkinson, *Zapata: A Biography*, 33.

Chapter 3

BRINGING THE REVOLUTION TO MORELOS

As the villagers from Villa de Ayala were sowing Anenecuilco's fields, Zapata returned from Mexico City, having been freed from his responsibilities as Ignacio's groom. Unwilling to allow his village to disappear, as it surely would have done if its citizens were deprived of a means to produce food and were forced to go elsewhere or become *peones* at nearby haciendas, Zapata gathered about 80 men to confront the Ayalans and the men from the hacienda Hospital who continued to guard the land. Guns in their hands, Zapata and his men told the Ayalans that he had no problem with them but that the land they were using was for Anenecuilcans. The Ayalans left, along with the outnumbered and outgunned hacienda guards. Zapata distributed lots to his village's people. The hacienda, at least at that point, didn't react, and Zapata's reputation began to spread throughout the region. From the start, the stories about him consisted of a mixture of truth and myth. Rosa King's hotel manager, Willie Nevin, for example, captured the spirit of Zapata's history if not its exact facts when he reported to his boss, "There's a fellow over near Cuautla-Emiliano Zapata's his name-who's been stirring up the people. It seems the hacienda annexed his father's *milpa*. Later they sent him to the owner's Mexico City house on an errand,

and when he saw the horses stabled there in marble stalls, it made him pretty sore."[1]

Zapata did not rest on his success. When the Hospital hacienda sought rent for the land later in 1910, he refused to pay it in Anenecuilco's name, explaining that the villagers had nothing to pay because the harvest had been bad that year. With the help of Refugio Yáñez, who was among those who had founded the Villa de Ayala's Leyvista club the previous year, Zapata defended the refusal at a hearing before the district *jefe*, José Vivanco, who ruled in Anenecuilco's favor. Vivanco, however, did not give Anenecuilco a complete victory, for he added that the village would have to pay some kind of rent in 1911. Zapata did not concede that provision of the ruling and appealed to Díaz to get the land permanently returned to the villagers. Díaz granted Anenecuilco's request, a concession that illustrates the changing nature of Mexico's political landscape in 1910, the year Díaz had claimed, in the Creelman interview, that he would allow someone else to become president.

Díaz did not honor his promise to retire. He set in motion the usual election process, one in which he was certain, as always, to win the presidency. The election was, nonetheless, different from the Díaz elections that had preceded it. Perhaps spurred by the example of opposition candidates in the gubernatorial election in Morelos—as well as the candidates that ran in elections in Sinaloa, Yucatán, and Coahuila— Francisco Indalecio Madero, a member of one of the wealthiest families in Mexico, set out to test the limits of Díaz's promises of real democratic elections. Madero had been involved in opposition politics before, founding his own party, the Club Benito Juárez, in 1904. He saw his involvement in politics as part of a spiritual journey, a fact that earned him the nickname the Apostle. He formed the *Centro Anti-reeleccionista de Mexico* (the Anti-Reelectionist Party) in May 1909, four months after he had published *La sucesion presidential en 1910* (*The Presidential Succession of 1910*), a book in which he argued that dictatorship prevented Mexicans from maturing and infected then with "corruption of the spirit, disinterest in public life, disdain for the law and a tendency toward dissimulation, cynicism and fear."[2]

In April 1910, the Anti-Reelectionist Party nominated Madero as its candidate to challenge Díaz for the presidency. Campaigning under the slogan *"Sufragio efectivo, no reeleccion"* ("Effective suffrage; No Reelection"),[3] the very slogan Díaz had used when he ran unsuccessfully for president in 1871, Madero met with a positive response, drawing "crowds of 25,000 and more supporters."[4] Realizing the threat he posed, Díaz had Madero arrested on June 13, eight days before Election Day, and the problem seemed to be solved. Díaz was so assured of his success that he allowed Madero, who had by this point concluded that armed revolt was the only way to bring reform to Mexico, to leave jail. Madero then snuck out of Mexico disguised as a railroad worker and began plotting Díaz's overthrow in San Antonio, Texas, where he drew up his Plan de San Luis Potosí. This document, which was named after the town in which he was jailed, declared Díaz's election void and named Madero the provisional Mexican president, though it promised that free elections would be held once Díaz was thrown out of office. On November 20, Madero crossed back into Mexico, expecting to find an army waiting for him to take control of three major cities—Mexico City, Puebla City, and Pachuca—but only a few supporters were waiting, the main players of the planned coup having been arrested in Mexico City in the days prior to Madero's return to the country. He, therefore, turned back and headed for New Orleans, where he considered his next move. Despite the failure of his plans, Madero had inspired uprisings in the north of Mexico, particularly the one led by another major revolutionary of the period, Pancho Villa, in the Chihuahua region, where the fighting was widespread enough to capture the attention of the press around the world. Villa, in fact, began his revolutionary career before Madero's plan was to come into effect, preparing for Madero's uprising by raiding the Chavarría hacienda, where he and his associates not only took horses, money, and other supplies but also killed Pedro Domínguez, the hacienda's administrator, when he resisted them.[5]

Rebellion in Morelos was taking a different form at this point. Zapata's success in standing up to the Hospital hacienda led nearby villages, Ayala and Moyotepec, to link their defense committees to Anenecuilco's, making Zapata the president of the joint Anenecuilco-Villa de Ayala-Moyotepec defense committee. He proceeded to take back communal lands from the haciendas in the two other villagers, and local authorities apparently feared to move against him. Indeed, even when

the hacendados managed to have Vivanco pushed out of his position—
after Zapata won the case related to Anenecuilco's lands—and got
Eduardo Flores, whom they thought would defend their interests more
strongly, appointed the local *jefe*, Zapata's activities went uncontested.
Riding out to confront Zapata over his redistribution of lands, Flores,
who had 10 men with him, found himself surrounded by about a hundred villagers under Zapata's command. Outnumbered, Flores could do
nothing but inquire if Zapata had joined the *Maderistas*, as was rumored
to be the case. Zapata not only denied the accusation but promised
to support the local authorities if *Maderistas* did become active in the
area. At the moment, he assured Flores, he was merely returning land
to its rightful owners. Flores could only allow him to continue his work,
turning Zapata, in effect, into the authority over land disputes in the
region.

Zapata's attention was not limited to local events. Despite the assurances he gave Flores, Zapata counted himself a member of a political
group that was considering joining the *Maderistas*. He must have understood, after all, that without radical change in the government, he
could not indefinitely stand up to the haciendas. The group—which
was made up of, among others, Rafael Merino, the son of the council
president whom Zapata replaced; Gabriel Tepepa, a 74-year-old Tlaquiltenango veteran of the French Intervention and the revolt that
brought Díaz to power; and Catarino Perdomo, who was from San
Pablo Hidalgo and would provide recruits for the Ayalan group when
it entered the revolution—met at Torres Burgos's home and discussed
the value of Madero's plan, debating its significance for Morelos. Torres
Burgos served as the leader at these meetings, although Zapata's influence on decisions was likely forceful. The group, after all, proceeded
with a caution typical of Zapata, a caution that he maintained in his
approach to using his newfound power in the region. Rather than flaunt
his successes, he attended to his business responsibilities, planting watermelons on his portion of the land that was taken back from Hospital
hacienda, when he wasn't helping those villages that had given him
authority to reappropriate land. Perhaps the biggest extravagance in
which he indulged was throwing a *jaripeo*—that is, a rodeo—for Vivanco when he left the region and attending another one in Moyotepec,

at which he injured his thigh. Participating in such events would have been ordinary for him in any case.

The main interest that Zapata and the others, if not all the members of the Ayalan group, had in Madero was a provision in his Plan de San Luis Potosí, which was mostly about political reform, that concerned returning communal land to villages. In the third article of his plan, Madero acknowledged that haciendas had been able to appropriate land with the help of "rulings of the Department of Public Development or by decisions of the tribunals of the Republic. As it is just to restore to their former owners the lands of which they were dispossessed in such an arbitrary manner, such rulings and decisions are declared subject to revision, and those who have acquired them in such an immoral manner, or their heirs, will be required to restore them to their former owners, to whom they shall also pay an indemnity for the damages suffered."[6] Zapata would not have treated words on a page as enough evidence for him to take up arms, and the group didn't either. Someone, it was decided, needed to discuss matters with Madero. In December, Torres Burgos went to San Antonio to meet with Madero and find out his intentions. Zapata thus waited, though such caution led Tepepa to break with the Ayalans when the wait came to seem too long. He began his uprising on February 7, 1911, but rejoined the Ayalan group the following month. Others in Morelos that were independent of the Ayalans also entered the revolution before Torres Burgos returned. Genovevo de la O, a figure well-known for opposing hacienda land grabs, had begun fighting in December 1910 and would remain independent of Zapata until 1912, and Bernabe Labastida, who had been sent to Quintana Roo for his participation in the Leyvista movement, took up arms in the area in which Tepepa was active in the latter part of February. The Ayalans risked getting involved too late for them to have any influence with the *Maderistas* should they succeed. Still, Zapata waited.

Torres Burgos returned home in mid-February 1911, bringing positive reports of Madero's intentions and assuming, under Madero's direction, command of the revolution in the south. Torres Burgos, Zapata, and Merino began planning to take up arms, making their final preparations on March 10 during an annual Lenten fiesta in Cuautla.

Zapata, who had been named a colonel, thought it was too early to join the fight, but the plan was enacted over his objections. On March 11, the conspirators arrived in Villa de Ayala, where they neutralized the local police and held an assembly in the village square. Torres Burgos read the Plan de San Luis Potosí, punctuating his reading with shouted revolutionary slogans. The crowd that had gathered followed his lead, having already shouted such slogans and fired shots into the air while Torres Burgos had been speaking. When the excitement died down, the now fully committed revolutionaries gathered about 70 men and headed toward southern Puebla, recruiting more men, including those whom Catarino Perdomo enlisted into the movement, along the way. At the time, recruitment was probably more difficult than it would become later on. Most of the leaders, including Zapata, lacked the reputation that would inspire the peasants with confidence. At the beginning of the revolution, as one peasant remarked, when Zapata began to be discussed, "we just criticized. Then you began to hear about Emiliano Zapata everywhere. It was Zapata this and Zapata that. But we said that he was only a peasant, not an intellectual."[7] Still, by the time the Ayalan rebels reached the safety of the mountains of Puebla on March 14, their force consisted of hundreds of volunteers, and more recruits arrived in the days that followed. Tepepa and his followers were among them.

The first major objective for the Ayalan led force was to capture Cuautla. It was, Torres Burgos probably suspected, the easiest major town to attack, as it was a center of Leyvista activity during the gubernatorial election and hence the place most likely to supply supporters. Zapata, nonetheless, felt it should not be attacked immediately because the volunteers, with the exception of Tepepa's, were ill-trained and ill-equipped. In fact, when Torres Burgos decided it was time for action a little more than a week after arriving in Puebla, Zapata objected, believing that the men needed more training before they would be ready to defeat the various village police or any federal troops that they might encounter. Torres Burgos, as leader, insisted that the campaign begin. The immediate aims were small. No attempt would be made to occupy towns; they would simply be entered, and weapons, supplies, and volunteers would be gathered. The tactic worked; there was little resistance. Indeed, Zapata's first sight of *federales*, at a train station in Axochiapan, Morelos, ended with the *federales'* retreating. Zapata, however, was not sent to the biggest immediate target, Jojutla, where Torres Burgos and Tepepa, who knew the area well, went. Zapata remained in the eastern part of Morelos, the area bordering Puebla around Jonacatepec.

The greater size of Torres Burgos and Tepepa's target did not prove problematic. Jojutla was briefly taken over by the rebel forces without a fight on March 24—exactly a week after Díaz had suspended the constitution and imposed martial law—but the subsequent looting of the town, as well as the freeing of prisoners from its jail, disturbed Torres Burgos. A junta, one in which Zapata participated, was then called to discuss the matter, but it refused to condemn the men's actions. Torres Burgos thus resigned from his position. While returning home, he and his two sons were surprised by *federales* and killed: their corpses were later displayed in Cuautla. The day Torres Burgos died, Zapata was voted in as the new leader of the revolutionary forces in Morelos. Zapata sought to legitimize this status by asking Octavio Magaña, a *Maderista* in the region on other business whom Zapata met by chance, to inform Madero that he had replaced Torres Burgos. While waiting for confirmation to arrive, Zapata's forces continued their raids, gathering volunteers and weapons. A typical raid, though perhaps made more dramatic by the use of a train, took place on March 28, when "the revolutionary forces drove a locomotive through the gates of Chinameca hacienda. Zapata and his men burst into the precincts and made off with forty Savage rifles, the whole ammunition supply, and all the hacienda's horses."[8] They saw little but success until the latter part of April, sometime after Juan Andrew Almazán, who styled himself a messenger from Madero—though whether he was or not is not known—arrived on April 4 and provided Zapata with official recognition. The first real defeat came near Izúcar de Matamoros, Puebla, when Zapata lost more than 100 followers, including Merino. His forces, by this point, had reached about 1,000 and were growing bigger by the day, while the number of federal forces shrank because troops had been removed to the north, where the situation seemed more serious.

Francisco Leyva, whom Díaz had appointed military commander of the state, now sought out Zapata to sign a treaty and discuss appointing a new governor, for Escandón had fled Morelos almost as soon as the fighting had begun. Zapata ignored the offer, determined to see the revolution succeed. Other leaders in the south, particularly Ambrosio Figueroa, were not as strong in their convictions. Figueroa was from Huitzuco, Guerrero, but began operating in Morelos to strengthen his position, as Morelos was closer to Mexico City. Establishing a base of power within it would place him closer to the country's political center. Zapata thus found himself contending with Figueroa for supremacy in Morelos, and the two made a nominal peace on April 22, signing the Pact of Jolalpan—a treaty that gave Zapata control over revolutionary activities in Morelos and Figueroa control in Guerrero—and arranging to launch a coordinated attack of Jojutla, which had been secured by the *federales* since the brief period in March when Zapata's *Maderistas* held it. Figueroa, however, also sought peace with the government, even reaching out to Díaz—an act that would lead Zapata to denounce him as a traitor in a letter to the press in Mexico City—and may have been plotting the assassination of Zapata and Tepepa, whom Figueroa would have killed on May 25 in Jojutla.

The assassination of Tepepa certainly lends credence to the concerns Zapata had about Figueroa's trustworthiness while preparing for the attack of Jojutla. Figueroa, Zapata came to believe, had made an agreement not to engage in battle with federal troops, which would have forced Zapata to face them alone. The capture of a man among Zapata's forces who was apparently employed by Figueroa to assassinate Zapata gave further credibility to the reports of Figueroa's dishonesty. The man was executed, and Zapata put the idea of attacking Jojutla behind him. He now began to consider how to improve his position within the *Maderista* movement, but he was interested in more than personal power. He wanted to improve his bargaining position in order to push for land reform once the revolution succeeded. To do that, he needed to achieve bigger victories and occupy territory. As April came to an end, having already taken Chietla and Izúcar de Matamoros, a town that the *federales* later took back, he began a siege of Jonacatepec in southeastern Morelos. Here, he used 2,000 men to drive out about 100 well barricaded soldiers, who, armed with machine guns, were able to hold off defeat for four days. Zapata sent line after line of cavalry toward the *federales'* positions, close to which Zapata's men tried to shoot the enemy and lasso their machine guns before getting killed. In the end, Zapata threatened to burn the town to the ground, and those soldiers who remained alive surrendered.

It is likely that Zapata introduced the use of dynamite boys during the siege of Jonacatepec.[9] These were young recruits who would saunter near enemy positions as if playing and then toss "[b]ombs made out of dynamite-filled tin cans"[10] through an opening. The explosions provided a signal for Zapata's horsemen to charge, the damage from the bombs giving them a greater chance to kill any of the enemy who remained alive. Harry H. Dunn describes such an attack in the following terms:

> Seven small boys, fourteen or fifteen years old, loitered in the plaza, Chasing each other, they crossed the little park, and began playing in the wide street in front of the barracks. All of them lighted [sic] long black cigars from one match. They spread out, one remaining before the open door, three on each side, running or playing leapfrog away from him. The door-guards watched them idly.
>
> Suddenly, the little fellows reached inside their ragged shirts. They withdrew small, round, bright objects, tin cans, with a short piece of string dangling from each. The boys touched these strings to the burning ends of their cigars, then hurled the round, bright objects at the *cuartel*. . . .
>
> A section of the roof rose into the air. The two guards disappeared. . . . Fragments of other men came through the gaping doorway.[11]

After the victory in Jonacatepec, coupled with the success of a force allied to him at Yautepec, Zapata began preparing for taking Cuautla, gathering about 4,000 men to face a strongly garrisoned town that was being defended by Mexico's Fifth Calvary Regiment, an elite force of about 400 that boasted that it had never been defeated. Zapata surrounded Cuautla by May 12 and began his attack the next day. The tactics that he had been using on garrisons were not as effective here, for the entrances to the streets and other open approaches to the city were covered by machine guns, making an approach with cavalry lines doomed to failure. Exchanges of fire did take place on the 13th, but

Zapata held off ordering a full attack until the 15th, after he had cut off the town's water supply. Still, the federal troops held their positions, and Zapata's casualties mounted. The next day, Zapata had gasoline poured into the aqueducts, in which *federales* held otherwise unreachable positions, and lit it. "This created," as Brunk writes, "a curtain of fire that quickly brought federals, many aflame, tumbling down."[12] At the same time, Zapata concentrated his troops more tightly as he sent them toward the city, and they eventually began taking out machine-gun positions closer to the ground. Over the next couple of days, the troops pushed their way closer to the town's center, wearing down the enemy with a constant barrage of gunfire and noise, which prevented the *federales* from sleeping. During the siege, General Leyva, who had been ordered to establish peace in Morelos, again sought out Zapata, this time asking for him to sign a peace treaty. Zapata replied, "You are no channel of authority for me, for I take orders only from the Provisional President of the Republic, Francisco Madero. . . . I only tell you that if you do not turn over Cuernavaca to me, I will have you shot."[13]

By the 19th, Zapata's troops neared the plaza, and dynamite boys were again put to use. The morale of the federal troops now wavered, leading them to abandon their posts as nightfall approached and head to Cuernavaca, where they arrived, as King described the scene, "Wounded, on foot, tied up in old rags they came. . . . Most of the men would never have made the thirty miles from Cuautla if it had not been for the help of their women, who had pushed them and dragged them along."[14] The siege had lasted a week and a large number, perhaps two thirds, of Zapata's army were either dead or wounded, but the losses were not in vain. They had helped Madero gain the upper hand in his negotiations with Díaz. The battle in Cuautla, the bloodiest of the Madero revolution by some accounts, had taken away any hopes that Díaz, as he admitted himself, might have had of retaining power. The battle demonstrated the need for his government to send significant numbers of troops to the south rather than concentrating a majority of them in the north, where the *Maderistas* had their strongest support.[15] Díaz would sign the Treaty of Ciudad Juarez two days after Cuautla fell, admitting defeat and agreeing to leave Mexico. On May 25, he officially resigned and left the country he had ruled for so long to live as an exile in France. His influence, however, remained. The treaty with Madero had made Francisco León de la Barra, "the nation's premier diplomat"[16] and a man not merely well adapted to the political culture developed by Díaz but a supporter of it, the interim president. The appointment illustrated that "continuity in many respects would prevail over change."[17]

Madero's respect for continuity would soon create difficulties for Zapata, even though in the immediate aftermath of the Cuautla victory, he found himself gaining prominence. He had gained national attention, which he may have hoped could be used to push Madero to carry out the agrarian reforms that had been discussed in the Plan de San Luis Potosí. The bloodiness of the victory also gave rise to the press's characterization of him as the Attila of the South and a leader of bandits, a charge that had been leveled against the original rebel force when it first began carrying out raids from the Puebla mountains and its men were said to be part of a revival of the *plateados*. That aspect of his reputation would create problems that his importance to Madero's victory, even though nationally recognized, would not overcome. Indeed, the reputation of his men for disorderliness and violence would plague him in the coming months, though the reports in the Mexico City papers were mostly propaganda. "[T]he Zapatistas . . . ," King would recall, "lived among us so peaceably for weeks."[18] Indeed, both the *federales* and Zapata's men were guilty of injustices against those who did not fight, but the memories of the locals suggest that the *federales* were worse from the beginning: "The government soldiers, and the rebel soldiers too, violated the young girls and the married women. They came every night and the women would give great shrieks when they were taken away," one woman recalled, but also noted, "The Zapatistas were well liked in the village, because although it is true they sometimes carried off young girls, they left the majority of the women in peace."[19] She went on to suggest that the revolutionary forces confined themselves to willing partners.

Events were overtaking Zapata; capturing Cuautla had taken too long, and by May 22, Figueroa, who had by this time signed a peace treaty with Leyva, had established control over Cuernavaca, which remained the center of political activity in Morelos. While Zapata fought in Cuautla, Figueroa sent forces to Cuernavaca under the

June 24, 1911: Zapata (seated, center) with (standing) Tirso Espinosa, Gildardo Magaña (second from left), Maurilio Mejía, Abráham Martínez, Jesús Jáuregui, Rodolfo Magaña, and (seated) Eufemio Zapata (left), and Próculo Capistran (right). (Library of Congress Prints & Photographs Division, LC-USZ62-73425)

command of Manuel Asúnsulo, an American-educated engineer who had joined Figueroa simply because of his proximity to him in Guerrero, and he served as the *Maderistas* representative in Cuernavaca in the immediate aftermath of Díaz's fall. Zapata did not arrive there until the 26th, by which time Asúnsulo had established his political presence. Asúnsulo, nevertheless, accommodated Zapata, joining with him to form a staff, which was headed by Abrahám Martínez, Zapata's secretary. Zapata and Martínez even began the process of picking a governor, writing three times to Alfredo Robles Domínguez, one of Madero's "peace commissioners,"[20] for permission to appoint one.[21] Meanwhile, Asúnsulo was politicking on his own, negotiating with Robles Domínguez, and proposed that Juan Carreón—a Cuernavaca banker who was originally from Chihuahua but had been the manager of the Bank of Morelos for six years—be made governor. Robles Domínguez concurred, allowing Carreón to assume the governorship on June 2.

Zapata had accepted, probably without enthusiasm, the appointment, sending Eufemio to representatives of Asúnsulo and Robles Domínguez to give his consent, but Carreón was not a trustworthy ally of Zapata, as his sympathies were with the hacendados. Before taking the governorship, he had even urged Robles Domínguez to keep Asúnsulo in Cuernavaca, noting that the better off citizens feared the disorder that Zapata's men had brought to it. Zapata, if he were aware of such concerns being raised, ignored the slight. He apparently accepted Carreón as governor to illustrate that he was willing to be cooperative and placed his hopes for reform on establishing a relationship with Madero, the commander whom he at that point thought he could trust to keep the promise to return the land to the people. Madero, however, was already backtracking on the idea of land reform, observing in his first post-revolutionary manifesto that the land-reform provisions in the Plan de San Luis Potosí "cannot be satisfied in all their amplitude."[22]

Whether or not he was aware of the new Madero manifesto, Zapata was in Mexico City on June 7 to meet Madero, and the two discussed the land issue the following day, after a dinner given in a house owned by Madero's family. Zapata insisted that the lands that had been taken from the villages be returned immediately so that the promise of the revolution could be fulfilled. Madero, for his part, noted the land issue was complicated and had to be resolved politically, not through violence, and said that Zapata's forces would first have to disarm. Zapata retorted, "Look, señor Madero, if I take advantage of the fact that I'm armed and take away your watch and keep it, and after a while we meet, both of us armed the same, would you have a right to demand that I give it back?" Madero replied that he would, and Zapata continued, "Well, that's exactly what has happened to us in Morelos, where a few planters have taken by force the villages' lands. My soldiers—the armed farmers and all the people in the villages—demand that I tell you, with full respect, that they want the restitution of their lands to be got underway right now."[23]

Madero made no definite promises and instead attempted to placate Zapata by offering him a hacienda, an offer he dismissed, proclaiming, "I did not join the Revolution in order to become a hacienda owner; if I am worth anything, it is because of the confidence and the trust which the farmers have in me."[24] The revolution was about reform, not personal gain. Still, Zapata tried to strengthen his alliance with Madero, inviting him to Morelos on June 12. The invitation back-fired, as Morelos' elites captured Madero's attention, convincing him that the reports of the barbarity of Zapata and his men were accurate. Zapata then seemed to be manipulated into disarming. The operation began on June 13 and was overseen by Zapata. His soldiers were paid to turn in their weapons, and 3,500 of them, for which the government had paid 47,500 pesos by June 21,[25] were turned in. These weapons may have consisted of less useful guns than had been used on the battle-fields, for Zapata's men, it was suspected, unloaded old weapons and kept their better rifles. Whether or not they were the actual weapons that had been used to defeat the *federales* is not known for certain, but Zapata would be able to quickly mobilize an armed force less than a month later. At the time, appearing to disarm was in Zapata's inter-ests, for Madero promised Zapata the post of commander of the state's police, an appointment the hacendados quickly set out to undermine through a propaganda war. Less than a week after Madero's departure from Morelos, the conservative paper *El Imparcial* printed an article that accused Zapata of, among other things, transforming Tepepa into a bandit and of terrifying the young women of Cuernavaca, three of whom Zapata was said to have raped himself. Many women, the report said, had fled the city. Zapata unwittingly aided the purpose of such propaganda by applying to Carreón to get guns from the states armory for his police force, although his appointment hadn't been made official—a point of ceremony that seemed irrelevant to Zapata. Car-reón refused the request, and Zapata took the weapons anyway. *El Imparcial* thus followed its earlier article with a piece titled "Za-pata is the Modern Attila," which described his removal of weapons from the armory as a raid, charged him with plotting to assassinate Figueroa and other figures, and credited him with asserting "the only government I recognize is my pistols."[26]

Zapata's position was now under threat. On June 20, he was back in Mexico City, meeting with Madero about the media reports. Zapata was able to convince Madero that the situation had been exaggerated in the press, but he also seemed to give up any pretensions that he had to power, agreeing to relinquish his appointment to become com-mander of the police and to retire from revolutionary activity. On his way home, waiting for a train in Mexico City, he informed a reporter for *El Pais,* "Now I'm going to work at discharging the men who helped me, so I can retire to private life and go back to farming my fields. For the only thing I wanted when I went into the revolution was to defeat the dictatorial regime, and this has been accomplished."[27] At that time, Zapata seems to have meant what he said. Events over the next five weeks, although not exactly encouraging to the cause of change, because the hacendados and other conservative figures continued to manipulate the situation to protect their interests, failed to convince him to change his mind. He even resisted calls for him to run for governor of Morelos, an idea that began as a grassroots movement but eventually gained the support of some of the more affluent in Morelos. Zapata's objection to taking the governorship could very well have been that the well-connected hoped to use him for symbolic purposes without allowing real change to take place. In any case, he got ready to settle down, marrying Josefa Espejo in a civil ceremony on July 28.[28] Troubles quickly pulled Zapata away from his domestic retirement and back into revolutionary activity.

NOTES

1. Rosa E. King, *Tempest over Mexico: A Personal Chronicle* (New York: Little Brown, 1940 [1935]), 59.

2. Quoted in Julia Preston and Samuel Dillon, *Opening Mexico: The Making of a Democracy* (New York: Farrar, Straus and Giroux, 2005), 46.

3. Ibid.

4. Michael J. Gonzales, *The Mexican Revolution, 1910–1940* (Albuquerque: University of New Mexico Press, 2002), 73.

5. For Villa's early revolutionary activities, see Friedrich Katz, *The Life and Times of Pancho Villa* (Stanford, CA: Stanford University Press, 1998), 76–77.

6. Quoted in *Revolutions in Mexico: Hearing Before a Subcommittee of the Committee on Foreign Relations, Senate Committee on Foreign Relations, 66th Congress* (1913), 733.

7. Quoted in Oscar Lewis, *Pedro Martínez: A Mexican Peasant and His Family* (New York: Random House, 1964), 87.

8. Adolfo Gilly, *The Mexican Revolution,* trans. Patrick Camiller (New York: New Press, 2006), 71.

9. Several sources, apparently on the authority of Harry H. Dunn, assert that Zapata used these boys in the siege of Yautepec, an attack that began with the use of dynamite boys. John Womack, *Zapata and the Mexican Revolution* (New York: Vintage Books, 1970 [1968]), see 85–86, and Samuel Brunk, *Emiliano Zapata! Revolution and Betrayal in Mexico* (Albuquerque: University of New Mexico Press, 1995), see 36, however, make clear that Zapata did not take part in that siege, suggesting Dunn misremembered the name of the town. See Harry H. Dunn, *The Crimson Jester: Zapata of Mexico* (New York: R. M. McBride, 1934), 49–50.

10. Philip S. Jowett, A. M. De Quesada, and Stephen Walsh, *The Mexican Revolution, 1910–20* (Oxford: Osprey, 2006), 18.

11. Dunn, *The Crimson Jester,* 49–50.

12. Brunk, *Emiliano Zapata!,* 38.

13. Quoted in Roger Parkinson, *Zapata: A Biography* (Briarcliff Manor, NY: Stein & Day, 1980 [1975]), 69.

14. King, *Tempest over Mexico,* 62.

15. See Frank McLynn, *Villa and Zapata: A History of the Mexican Revolution* (New York: Carroll & Graf, 2002), 94.

16. Peter V. N. Henderson, *In the Absence of Don Porfirio* (Wilmington, DE: Scholarly Resources, 2000), 15.

17. Ibid., 23.

18. King, *Tempest over Mexico,* 76.

19. Quoted in Oscar Lewis, *Pedro Martínez: A Mexican Peasant and His Family* (New York: Random House, 1964), 92.

20. Henderson, *In the Absence of Don Porfirio,* 58.

21. Ibid., 86.

22. Quoted in Womack, *Zapata and the Mexican Revolution,* 90.

23. Quoted in Womack, *Zapata and the Mexican Revolution,* 96. Henderson has recently argued that Zapata's analogy was "not quite apt. . . . The planters had not taken possession of the villagers' land by force of arms; instead they had legal title, or at least legal color of title" (*In the Absence of Don Porfirio,* 88). Henderson seems to ignore the fact that the haciendas enforced their land grabs with the arms of the *rurales* and, sometimes, of their own men. The hacienda Hospital, for

example, used its employees to guard the fields of Anenecuilco in the spring of 1910. To be fair to Henderson, he is articulating the probable point of view of Madero and the interim government that was put into place after Díaz's fall but before Madero's election. The divide separating Zapata's and Madero's views points to a fundamental division in how the different parties regarded the purpose of the revolution. Zapata saw victory as a negation of the old order, whereas Madero saw it as a condemnation of the figures who controlled that order.

24. Quoted in John David Ragan, *Emiliano Zapata* (New York: Chelsea House, 1989), 39.

25. Henderson, *In the Absence of Don Porfirio*, 88.

26. Quoted in Brunk, *Emiliano Zapata!*, 46.

27. Quoted in Womack, *Zapata and the Mexican Revolution*, 128.

28. See Womack for this date for the civil ceremony (*Zapata and the Mexican Revolution*, 107n1); Parkinson dates the civil ceremony June 26, see *Zapata: A Biography*, 92.

Chapter 4

THE REVOLUTION CONTINUES AND THE PLAN DE AYALA

On the night of August 9, 1911, Zapata was celebrating his marriage—which had been solemnized earlier in the day in a religious ceremony at a Catholic Church—but forces were gathering to draw him away from the domestic peace that he was attempting to establish. Such forces had been pushing Zapata toward taking up arms again for more than a month. On July 5, an incident revolving around a Madero visit to Puebla put Zapata's intention to retire to the test. Rumors that an attempt to assassinate Madero was being planned for his visit led Abrahám Martínez to arrest a federal deputy and some state officials, among other suspects. Martínez was then arrested for assuming the authority of the federal government, and fighting between *federales* and *Maderistas*, specifically the elements within the movement that could be identified as Zapata's followers, led to the death of more than 50 people. Zapata quickly mobilized forces in Morelos with the intention of heading to Puebla from Cuautla but was told to stay where he was. When Madero arrived on the scene on July 13, he took the side of the *federales*, blaming Martínez for stirring up trouble. Zapata returned home, and although his men remained prepared should problems arise and new recruits began to join his forces, he focused his energies on settling down, working his fields, preparing to resume horse breeding, and organizing his religious wedding.

Zapata, of course, remained interested in the direction de la Barra was taking the country, concerned that the revolutionaries' efforts had been for nothing and that one regime that favored the hacendados was simply being replaced with another one. In Morelos, as in many parts of Mexico, the hacendados were reconsolidating their power, something they were able to do because of the policy under de la Barra—a policy with which Madero agreed—to disarm the citizens so as to guarantee their adherence to the government's laws. Zapata was keeping his forces armed, in fact, to protect the gains that the campesinos had made since the summer of 1910. Still, armed conflict wasn't, he seemed to realize, in the best interest of Morelos, and he sought peaceful means to protect the principles of the revolution. When a group of *Maderistas* met with de la Barra on July 18 to complain that the Plan de San Luis Potosí was not being implemented, Zapata thus sent representatives to speak for Morelos, and on July 22, he signed, along with other dissatisfied revolutionary generals, a protest against de la Barra's provisional government. Madero, hoping to smooth out the disagreement with Zapata, attempted to set up a meeting with him at the spa of Tehuacán in Puebla. Zapata refused the invitation, first telling Madero that he was ill and later claiming that he feared that enemies of the revolution might seize on the opportunity to have them both assassinated. The truth was that Zapata had already begun to distrust Madero—despite publicly defining him as "the only man in whom all the hopes and aspirations of the Mexican people have been placed"[1] early in August. Zapata did finally send Eufemio, who had joined him when the fighting broke out and remained in Morelos thereafter, but nothing was accomplished at that meeting.

De la Barra would soon force Zapata's hand. Stepping up efforts to disarm Zapata's men, de la Barra pushed Emilio Vásquez Gómez, a Zapata ally who had denied Juan Carreón's request for extra federal troops back in June and likely supplied new weapons to Zapata in July, to resign as the minister of the interior and placed Alberto García Granados in that position. García Granados, a Puebla planter, assumed a harder stance against the existence of Morelos's armed militia. Taking the position that "[t]he government does not deal with bandits," García Granados ordered Zapata to disarm his men immediately or face the onslaught of federal troops. Zapata ignored the order, continuing to go about his private business as if giving up an active role in the revolution were his genuine intention, even as his defiance with regard to disarming left those in the central government distrustful.

García Granados, with the support of de la Barra, backed up his threat, sending Victoriano Huerta, a Porfirian general known for his brutality, to Morelos with more than a thousand troops on August 9. In the midst of his wedding celebrations, Zapata was informed by a messenger about Huerta's arrival. He left the festivities, immediately writing to Madero, "Do you have any complaints against me?"[2] and demanding the withdrawal of Huerta's troops, who were already in Cuernavaca. Figueroa, who had been offered the governorship of Morelos that day, was waiting to join Huerta's forces with his own troops with the blessing of Madero, who had written to Figueroa and told him, "Put Zapata in his place for us, since we can no longer stand him." In the following days, Zapata's forces prepared to defend themselves as best they could. Squabbling between Huerta—who seems to have wanted the situation to escalate so that Zapata could be crushed militarily—and Morelos's leaders, as well as a disagreement between Madero and de la Barra over how to handle the situation, provided Zapata more time for preparations. The quarrelling also led Figueroa to refuse, at least for the time being, the governorship.

Madero had second thoughts about using troops against Zapata's men, perhaps because it was rumored that Huerta was working in the service of Bernardo Reyes, a conservative-thinking presidential hopeful whose secretary was travelling with Huerta. Deciding to attempt to bring a peaceful resolution to the situation, Madero traveled to Cuernavaca on August 13, a day after Genovevo de la O, who was not yet acting under the leadership of Zapata but who objected to the presence of the *federales*, attacked Huerta's men and de la Barra declared martial law in the state. Madero sought to negotiate with Zapata, writing to him and asking him to come to Cuernavaca. Zapata stayed where he was but spoke with Madero over the phone. Zapata, while insisting his intentions were to retire, demanded that the federal troops be removed from the region, that a governor who accepted the principles of the revolution be appointed, and that a revolutionary force should remain armed "to take custody of the state's public security while a legislature is elected, which . . . will settle or solve the matter which occupies us—the agrarian matter."[3] At the same time, Zapata sent de la Barra a warning, telling him, "The people want their rights respected. They want to be paid attention to and listened to. Just because they make a protest, nobody can try to shut them up with bayonets."[4]

Madero, after two days of discussions, which involved selecting a replacement for Governor Carreón, came to an agreement with Zapata and sent de la Barra a telegram about the settlement on August 15. That same day, de la Barra told Huerta to move forward with his plans and to tell Madero that if Zapata's forces did not disarm, the *federales* would move into Yautepec, which was about 10 miles from Cuautla. Madero was not told about de la Barra's new orders, and as soon as Madero left Cuernavaca for Mexico City on August 16, Huerta moved his troops onto the road toward Yautepec, believing a show of force would compel Zapata to follow through with his promise to disarm.

De la Barra began to reconsider his options after receiving a telegram from Madero, one that arrived a day later than it should have. It explained the disadvantages of confronting Zapata with military might. Doing so, Madero reasoned, could lead to an extended conflict. Zapata, after all, already had about a thousand followers mobilized and could quickly gather more if he needed to do so. Moreover, other *Maderistas* were more likely to join Zapata than to provide assistance to the federal army, against which they had recently fought. Finding a peaceful solution to the problem was thus the safest thing to do. Madero returned to Cuautla on August 18—embracing Zapata and calling him his "truest general"[5] upon his arrival—with the hope of concluding the negotiations, even though an attack on Jojutla by men thought to be members of Zapata's army the previous day and the subsequent sacking of the town threatened to derail any peaceful solution to the impasse. Zapata was, for the most part, agreeable, accepting Madero's terms, which included allowing Eduardo Hay, a former aide to Madero and revolutionary general from the north, to become governor, even though Zapata had earlier made a point about putting men from Morelos in charge of the state government. He also agreed to the appointment of Madero's brother Raúl to the post of police commander and to the use of

250 revolutionaries from Hidalgo, who had already been absorbed into the federal army, for a peace-keeping force in the region. Disarmament would begin the following day under the direction of *Maderistas* rather than federal troops.

One issue, Huerta's continued presence, complicated the situation. Zapata did not want to disarm so long as *federales* were in Morelos, whereas de la Barra wanted the presence of the *federales* to insure Zapata's compliance with his orders, believing that the threat of force had brought Zapata to the negotiation table in the first place. The attack on Jojutla provided de la Barra with an excuse to allow Huerta to stay put. Zapata seemed to place his faith in Madero, beginning to demobilize on August 19. De la Barra remained distrustful, believing an informant's report that Zapata did not intend to give up his arms and would merely repeat the ruse he had carried out in June, relinquishing useless weapons while keeping the better ones hidden or arranging to reacquire weapons as he had done in June. De la Barra thus ordered Huerta to continue his march toward Yautepec. The general arrived there on August 20 and soon became involved in a short skirmish with Zapata's men, an incident that led Madero to rush to Yautepec to contain the situation. Zapata followed him and again affirmed his commitment to the agreement that the two had just signed.

Madero convinced de la Barra to halt Huerta's progress for two days, during which time Zapata was to demobilize his forces completely. At least, that's what Zapata was told and what Madero perhaps believed, but stopping the progress of the *federales* for two days wasn't really a concession: Huerta needed that long to prepare the road for the heavy artillery he had. At the same time, Figueroa was sent to the border region around Puebla to prevent disturbances such as the one in Jojutla a few days earlier. Zapata then restarted demobilizing his forces, though questions about the validity of the effort remained for de la Barra and Huerta. Huerta went so far as to tell de la Barra that the only real solution to the problem was "to reduce Zapata to the last extremity, even hang him or throw him out of the country."[6] On August 23, the road having been cleared, Huerta advanced toward Cuautla, apparently on his own initiative. The move enraged Zapata and his men; Eufemio even called for Madero to be shot as a traitor. Madero was also angry, and he returned to Mexico City to plead with de la Barra to order

Huerta to stop his advance. The next day, Huerta was told to stay in Yautepec, although Casso López, another Porfirian general who would take over operations in Morelos later in the year, was sent to Cuautla from Jonacatepec. De la Barra soon decided he had waited long enough and ordered Huerta, along with Figueroa and López, to pacify Morelos through force.

De la Barra's attempt to find a military solution began the next day, and any hope that Zapata would reconcile with the provisional government came to an end. De la Barra went so far as to have criminal charges filed against Zapata and to order his arrest. On August 27, Zapata—having grabbed what supplies he could and fled Cuautla with the personal guard that his agreement with Madero had allowed him to keep—published his response, a manifesto called "To the People of Morelos" that condemned the government's aggression and defended his own position. Two days later, Zapata would again reach out to de la Barra, protesting that the blood that was about to be shed was the responsibility of the government. Zapata had, at least as he saw it, made an agreement with Madero in good faith and had been attacked for his trouble. Distrustful of Zapata and therefore uninterested in compromise, de la Barra informed Huerta of Zapata's location, the hacienda Chinameca, where Huerta and López, both occupying Cuautla by that point, headed.

On September 1, Zapata faced his first attack, although it came from neither Huerta nor López. Figueroa, as displeased as anyone about Huerta's occupying Morelos, which he now regarded as his territory, sent Federico Morales after Zapata. Morales arrived at Chinameca first and stormed its front gate, but without first surrounding the property. Zapata was thus able to slip out the back, escaping through sugarcane fields. Seventy-two hours later, he was in the mountains of Puebla, where he ran into Juan Andrew Almazán, and the two began devising their response. Over the next couple of weeks, Zapata laid low. Huerta imposed order on all six districts of Morelos, and by the end of the month, he believed he had achieved victory. Figueroa, despite his resentment over Huerta's presence in Morelos, accepted the governorship of the state and also the position of military commander. Morelos was apparently under government control. Huerta's approach to imposing order, however, had created more problems than it had solved, giving Zapata an advantage that few outside Morelos understood. The hacendados, as well as the peasants, saw what the provisional government did not, that Huerta's strong-arm tactics—"sowing trust, if the word fits, with the rifles and with the cannon of the Government of the Republic,"[7] as he described them himself in a letter to de la Barra—turned the campesinos, former *Maderistas* as well as those who had previously acted as mere observers, against the federal government and into *Zapatistas*, a category that had only come into being as separate from *Maderistas* in the weeks following Huerta's arrival in the state.

That Zapata remained at large gave the lie to Huerta's pretensions to victory, and on the same day that Huerta had declared Morelos pacified, September 26, Zapata issued his second manifesto, a document signed by him, his brother, and twelve others. Although it acknowledged the legitimacy of de la Barra's provisional government, the manifesto demanded the removal of the governor of Morelos, as well as the governors of Puebla, Guerrero, and Oaxaca, states in which Zapata had found support among disenfranchised *Maderistas* in the preceding weeks. The governors were to be replaced, the manifesto went on to say, with candidates chosen in free elections or with men picked by the generals and chiefs—that is, those who signed the document—of what they were inaccurately calling the Counterrevolution. The document also called for the removal of federal troops from the four states; the postponement of the presidential elections; the release of all political prisoners; and the return of land, as well as water and timber rights, to the villages. De la Barra, who offered amnesty to "political refugees" but not those who had been declared criminals—that is, Zapata—ordered Huerta to go to San Juan del Rio, Puebla, where Zapata had indicated he was located, and put an end to such posturing.

Huerta left Cuernavaca on September 27. Confident that Zapata would be easily captured, he told Mrs. King, "he would be back in two or three days with the prisoner on exhibition."[8] Zapata proved a trickier adversary: he was prepared for Huerta's arrival—likely having revealed his location in order to bring the general into the mountains of Puebla—for he had spies stationed in Morelos who sent him reports of Huerta's movements. When Huerta reached Puebla, his troops clashed with the *Zapatistas*, who retreated after short skirmishes. They repeated that pattern of fight and retreat for a short time and then changed tactics, retreating as soon as Huerta's forces came into view. Huerta was thus drawn higher into the mountains, a territory with which he and his soldiers had little familiarity. Taking advantage of their greater knowledge of the region, Zapata and about 250 of his men slipped around the federal troops and, riding fast, emerged in eastern Morelos 24 hours later. Over the next few days, Zapata stepped up recruitment. Those who had fought with him the previous spring, as well as those who had suffered as a result of Huerta's activities in Morelos in September, now joined the *Zapatistas,* and by October 10, the force had swelled to 1,500 men and was continuing to grow.

Huerta was still in Puebla, but Zapata, in some respects, remained cautious, limiting his actions to what amounted to raids on such places as Axochiapan and Tenextepango rather than attempting to occupy towns. In another respect, he showed a brazenness that would instill deep concern among the nation's elite. He moved north, leaving the confines of Morelos behind him and entering the federal district of Mexico City, where he attacked and briefly occupied the Milpa Alta garrison. Zapata's entering of the federal district, even if it didn't change his position, had immediate political effects. De la Barra felt the need to shake up his cabinet, and he forced several ministers, including García Granados, to resign. For his part, Madero was able to insist that de la Barra dismiss Huerta. More strikingly, the date of Madero's inauguration was moved forward. Madero, who had easily defeated de la Barra, as well as Reyes, in the October 1 presidential election, was to be sworn into office on December 1, 1911: Zapata's boldness had led the date of the ceremony to be changed to November 6.

Zapata's success over the month of October had once again transformed the nature of his public persona. Although he was still regarded as a bandit by the government and the press, he had become something much more important to the campesinos. They may have learned to admire him before, but they now looked upon him as a figure behind whom they could rally and seek what they thought the revolution should have brought them. As the congressman José María Lozano, during a debate in congress over what to do about Zapata, declared, "Emiliano Zapata is no longer a man, he is a symbol. He could turn himself in tomorrow . . . but the rabble [following him] . . . would not surrender."[9]

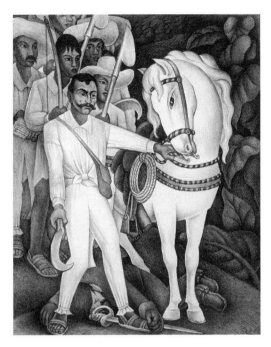

Diego Rivera's lithographic portrait of Zapata, backed by armed peasants, standing over the body of an enemy of the revolution, circa 1932. (Library of Congress, Prints & Photographs Division)

Madero assured the nation that when he took his office, he would be able to rein in Zapata, proclaiming in a public letter that "Zapata would lay down his arms because 'he knows that I will carry out the earlier propositions of the government,'" that is, carry through on the terms of the agreement that had been negotiated in August, "which I believe are the only means of pacifying the state of Morelos."[10] That Madero's assurance would be carried through with seemed very likely after the inauguration ceremony. By that point, Zapata had already begun a ceasefire—returning, along with his men, to Villa de Ayala and ordering his followers to allow the railways and telephone and telegraph lines that they had destroyed to be repaired throughout Morelos—and Alfredo Robles Domínguez was dispatched to negotiate peace, arriving in Cuautla on November 8. By November 11, Robles Domínguez had worked out a new agreement with Zapata, one very like the one that Madero had made in August. It called for the *Zapatistas* to replace, gradually, the *federales* in Morelos; the agrarian reforms for which Zapata had initially taken up arms to be instituted; and the actions of those who had fought with Zapata in recent months to be sanctioned as legitimate.

The new agreement, however, was being threatened even before it had been worked out. During the three days in which Zapata and Robles Domínguez negotiated, General Casso López, following his orders to disarm the *Zapatistas* from de la Barra that had never been withdrawn, moved in, surrounding Zapata's forces in Villa de Ayala and then attempting to prevent Robles Domínguez from leaving for Mexico City once negotiations had been concluded. When he did manage to evade the *federales* and get to Mexico City, Robles Domínguez found that the situation had changed. Madero, perhaps fearing his authority would be undermined by giving in to a man most people in the country considered a bandit, had changed his mind and now refused to sanction, publicly at least, any agreement. Robles Domínguez was sent back to Morelos with the following instructions:

> Let Zapata know that the only thing I can accept is that he immediately surrender unconditionally and that all his soldiers immediately lay down their arms. In this case I will pardon his soldiers for the crime of rebellion and he will be given passports so that he can go and settle temporarily outside the state. Inform him that his rebellious attitude is damaging my government greatly and that I cannot tolerate that it continue under any circumstances, that if he truly wants to serve me, to obey me is the only way he can do it. Let him know that he need fear nothing for his life if he lays down his arms immediately.[11]

Madero did apparently ask Robles Domínguez to offer Zapata, in private, better conditions for his surrender, but that message was never delivered. Casso López refused Robles Domínguez access to Villa de Ayala, where Zapata was making preparations to defend against the *federales'* imminent attack and only received the public instructions and a vague letter from Robles Domínguez about other arrangements. Zapata dismissed the messenger, Gildardo Magaña, shortly before the *federales* began firing their artillery. Then he ordered most of his men, no match for the superior weapons of the federal army, to retreat. He remained in Villa de Ayala until the evening, when he and the few men that he had kept with him as an escort slipped out of the region and returned to the Puebla mountains, gathering recruits as they made their way.

For the next few weeks, Zapata—who around this same time proclaimed, "I am resolved to struggle against everything and everybody"[12]—developed the Plan de Ayala with Otilio Montaño, who is credited with writing the document. It was issued at the end of November from Ayoxustla, a small town in southeastern Puebla, where Zapata's chiefs had gathered to hear the details.[13] The Plan, divided into 15 sections, begins by making its case against Madero, who "through lack of integrity and the highest weakness, did not carry to a happy end the revolution which gloriously he initiated with the help of God and the people, since he left standing most of the governing powers and corrupted elements of oppression of the dictatorial government of Porfirio Díaz . . . [and] tries to avoid the fulfillment of the promises which he made to the Nation in the Plan of San Luis Potosí."[14] Zapata went on to proclaim that his revolution will make Madero's plan its own, although in a slightly modified form. General Pascual Orozco, a *Maderista* commander in the north, was named as the new revolution's chief, though Zapata, it was explained, would assume the position should Orozco decline it. The meat of the document is contained in sections six, seven, and eight, where the *Zapatista* version of land reform, defined as "an additional part" of Madero's plan, is clearly outlined. The first of these sections proclaims that land appropriated from the villages will be returned to those who hold the original titles. The next states that a third of the land held by large landowners will be confiscated and distributed among the villages, or pueblos, and ordinary citizens so that impoverished Mexicans will have the opportunity to improve their conditions. The last concerns those landowners who oppose the *Zapatista* reform; their entire estates will be confiscated. Two-thirds of such estates, the part that the owners would have been allowed to keep, would be sold and used "for indemnizations of war [and] pensions for widows and orphans of the victims who succumb in the struggle for the present plan."[15]

The plan helped to bring a number of anti-Madero chiefs together under the *Zapatista* banner, perhaps the most important of which in the immediate context of 1911 was Genovevo de la O, whose independent revolutionary activity had been carried out on a large scale already. Other chiefs included Maurilio Mejía, a nephew of Zapata; Amador Salazar, a cousin who had spent time in the army as a draftee; Felipe Neri, who had lost his hearing during the siege of Cuautla when a homemade bomb exploded near him; Fortino Ayaquica, a textile worker who had been involved with the Partido Liberal Mexicano (PLM); and Jesús "One-Eyed" Morales, a Puebla bar owner and occasional bandit prior to the revolution. At this point, the *Zapatistas* were held together—though not always—by the perception of a common cause. They lacked a steady source of income and weapons, relying on donations from supporters or on what could be captured in raids. Furthermore, the movement was disorganized in some ways: Zapata had no secure center of operations; he moved from temporary camp to temporary camp to avoid being captured or killed, and each chief, or general, was left to operate in his own area of Morelos in a semi-independent fashion.

Despite the limited reach of its soldiers, the threat of *Zapatismo* was recognized in Mexico City. In December, Madero—who countenanced the publication of the Plan de Ayala in a Mexico City paper on December 15 so that all could see "how crazy Zapata is"[16]—again attempted to make peace, though on his own terms, offering Zapata nothing more than to be allowed to live in exile. He roundly rejected the offer, complaining, "I've been Señor Madero's most faithful partisan. I've given infinite proofs of it. But I'm not any more. Madero has betrayed me as well as my army, the people of Morelos, and the whole nation. . . . [N]obody trusts him any longer because he has violated all his promises. He's the most fickle, vacillating man I've ever known." Zapata went on to promise, "in a month, I'll be in Mexico City with twenty thousand men, and have the pleasure of going up to Chapultepec castle and dragging him [Madero] out of there and hanging him from one of the highest trees in the park."[17] Such threats were rhetorical at that point, but Zapata's efforts to gain strength were again helped by the government and the strong-armed approach its general, now Casso López, continued to use to stamp out rebellion. The support Zapata would get was not unconditional and was threatened by the activity of bandits, some of whom were *Zapatistas*, whereas others were simply operating under the guise of being revolutionaries.

NOTES

1. Quoted in Samuel Brunk, *Emiliano Zapata! Revolution and Betrayal in Mexico* (Albuquerque: University of New Mexico Press, 1995), 51.

2. Quoted in Roger Parkinson, *Zapata: A Biography* (Briarcliff Manor, NY: Stein & Day, 1980 [1975]), 96.

3. Ibid., 98.

4. Quoted in John Womack, *Zapata and the Mexican Revolution* (New York: Vintage Books, 1970 [1968]), 115.

5. Ibid., 116.

6. Quoted in Alan Knight, *The Mexican Revolution*, vol. 2 (Lincoln: University of Nebraska Press, 1990), 263.

7. Quoted in Parkinson, *Zapata: A Biography*, 108.

8. Rosa King, *Tempest over Mexico: A Personal Chronicle* (New York: Little Brown, 1940 [1935]), 86.

9. Womack, *Zapata and the Mexican Revolution*, 123.

10. Stanley Robert Ross, *Francisco I. Madero: Apostle of Mexican Democracy* (New York: Columbia University Press, 1955), 201.

11. Quoted in Frank McLynn, *Villa and Zapata: A History of the Mexican Revolution* (New York: Carroll & Graf, 2002), 119.

12. McLynn, *Villa and Zapata*, 120.

13. Many sources date the issuance of the plan as November 28, 1911. (See, for example, Anita Brenner and George R. Leighton, *The Wind That Swept Mexico: The History of the Mexican Revolution of 1910–1942* [Austin: University of Texas Press, 2008 (1943)], 302), although the date affixed to it is November 25, 1911 (see Plan de Ayala, trans. John Womack, http://www.hist.umn.edu/~rmccaa/la20c/ayala.htm).

14. Plan de Ayala, trans. John Womack http://www.hist.umn.edu/~rmccaa/la20c/ayala.htm.

15. Ibid.

16. Parkinson, *Zapata: A Biography*, 96.

17. Quoted in Womack, *Zapata and the Mexican Revolution*, 127.

.

Chapter 5

IN THE FACE OF BRUTALITY AND GENTLENESS

Although attacking Mexico City with 20,000 troops in the immediate future remained unrealistic for the *Zapatistas*, establishing a space for themselves in Morelos turned out to be well within their capabilities. One of the first things they did was to make their forces more professional. Zapata introduced, at the end of 1911—probably at the same time the Plan de Ayala was drafted—a command structure that brought a sense of cohesion to his army. He was now styled general-and-chief, while his brother Eufemio served as the chief of seven generals, who were, in turn, in command of 27 colonels, as well as a number of captains, other officers, and soldiers.[1] On December 20, 1911, Zapata was thus able to issue commands to the entire Liberating Army of the South—a designation that the *Zapatistas* had taken over from the rebels who had organized in support of Madero earlier in the year—as a whole. The commands were not military in nature. Rather, they illustrated Zapata's desire to respect the social order, at least the elements of it that he regarded as legitimate, which included, to some degree, the haciendas. He also sought to counteract the damage that banditry could cause his movement. Zapata instructed his officers "to respect and aid civil authorities who have been legally and freely elected" and not to "destroy or burn the property of the haciendas, because these will be the patrimony and source of work for the villages." He understood, "the better we behave, the more adherents and help we will have among the people." The importance of the regular soldiers to the traditional order even took precedence over their importance to the rebellion, for those who were needed at home for the harvest were to be granted discharges. More publicly, Zapata issued a manifesto condemning banditry or those who commit outrages in his name and asking "all my partisans and the pueblos in general to throw back [such persons] with energy, for these I consider enemies of mine who try to discredit our blessed cause and prevent its triumph."[2]

By the time those orders were issued, the *Zapatistas* had gained momentum, and as the year came to a close, government forces were in control of the region in name only. They maintained a firm hold on the towns in which their troops were stationed, but the *Zapatistas* were, if not in control of the areas outside those towns, able to operate freely in the countryside. Rebels, under the direct command of Genovevo de la O, were even threatening Cuernavaca, and they came close to taking the city in January 1912. They were slowed down, but not defeated, at the end of the month. Events elsewhere also contributed to gains in Morelos, for rebellion, inspired in part by the success of the *Zapatistas*, spread to such states as Tlaxcala, Puebla, Michoacán and Guerrero, preventing the government from focusing its energies solely on Morelos. Figueroa resigned as governor, pleasing even Madero loyalists, who had been unhappy with his governorship and hoped a local would be named to take his place. Two days later, on January 19, martial law was declared for four months. That move did little to thwart the rebels or undermine the support that they received: a journalist for a Mexico City paper reported at the end of January, "I have become convinced that Zapatism has spread to an extraordinary degree. All the small villages are on the side of Emiliano Zapata. Major centers like Tepalcingo support his forces and greet them with abundant supplies, whereas they display a hostile attitude to government troops and refuse them everything."[3]

Altering the hostile atmosphere in Morelos for the benefit of the government remained a possibility, and Madero's appointment of Francisco Naranjo, Jr., an early supporter of the revolution in northern Mexico, as the new interim governor could have proved an effective means, if not to sway Zapata and others like him to give up their struggle, to undermine support for rebels in the region. Naranjo genuinely seemed to want to find solutions for the problems facing Morelos's communities, observing, after a short analysis of the region's problems, "I found that Morelos lacked three things—first ploughs, second books and third equity. And it had more than enough latifundias, taverns and bosses."[4] Indeed, the goodwill he sought to create eventually chipped away at the support that the *Zapatistas* had gained as a result of the indifference of Figueroa, whose aspirations were personal, and the brutality of Huerta and Casso López. But the direction the government took at the start of Naranjo's term was beyond his control. Naranjo's efforts to bring peace to the state, however, did have some help early on from those in Mexico City. Madero's brother Gustavo arranged for Abrahám Martínez and two others from Zapata's inner circle, Gildardo and Rodolfo Magaña, to be released from jail near the end of January. Hoping for reconciliation with Zapata, Gustavo, who knew at that point that Pascual Orozco had privately broken with Madero and would soon stage his own uprising in Chihuahua, tried to use the released prisoners as negotiators, telling them, during a private meeting, that Zapata's actions were not without reason and it was "our duty to try again for a reconciliation."[5]

Gustavo's attempts to arrange for some kind of peace came to an end when the three men he sent to Morelos rejoined the *Zapatistas*. In the meantime, Naranjo's work was undermined by the crisis of the rebellion, along with an unimaginative approach to ending it. De la O, for example, was again threatening Cuernavaca in February, and, on February 9, the *federales* attacked de la O's hometown, Santa María, burning it and its surroundings to the ground and killing de la O's daughter in the process. Such brutality hardened the resistance, and Naranjo had little power to stop it. He was also forced to maintain the status quo in other ways, for example, keeping the previous lieutenant governor, Aurelio Velázquez—at least until he was forced to resign after being accused of supporting anti-Madero elements in the region at the beginning of March—and turning a blind eye to such abuses of power as the expulsion of locals from town councils. More damaging to Naranjo's efforts to address the problems facing Morelos was Madero's

decision to send Brigadier General Juvencio Robles, who would sur-
pass the brutality of the generals sent before him through a policy that
willfully ignored differences among various groups in Morelos, to put
an end to *Zapatismo*. Before his arrival in the region in early February,
Robles demonstrated that his view of the problem was almost certain
to lead him to increase tensions in the state, declaring, "All Morelos,
as I understand it, is *zapatista*, and there's not a single inhabitant who
doesn't believe in the false doctrines of the bandit Emiliano Zapata."[6]

When he arrived, Robles immediately intensified the battle against
the *Zapatistas*, going after anyone he believed to be associated with
the movement, no matter how tangential that association might be to
actual subversive activities. Zapata's sister Luz, as well as his mother-
in-law and two sisters-in-law, were arrested in what seems to have been
a symbolic gesture, and a policy of resettlement was put into effect on
February 15. That policy involved relocating people who might prove
allies to Zapata from their homes to concentration camps close to large
towns, where they could be more easily monitored. The practice was a
standard method of fighting guerrillas for the Mexican army, but Robles
went beyond simply forcing people from their homes. Turning the actions that had been taken against de la O's village into a statewide
policy, he decreed that the villages were to be burned to the ground
after they were emptied so that they could not be used as hideouts by
rebels later on. The first village to suffer such a fate was Nexpa. Women
and children, for the most part, were the only ones remaining within
the village on the day it was attacked; all were arrested and moved to
housing outside of Jojutla, where they were forced to remain even after
being released from custody. Other villages that suffered similar fates
include San Rafael, Ticumán, and Los Hornos. The latter village was
the only one that had a direct connection to the resistance: one of
Zapata's headquarters was hidden in it. Houses in Villa de Ayala were
also burned, and more villages were soon added to the list of those destroyed, all before the end of February. During this same period, *peones*
or campesinos could be and were shot simply for being suspected of
supporting or belonging to the *Zapatistas*, that is, for being in the open
countryside rather than in a concentration camp.

Robles proceeded, practically unchecked, for about six weeks—only
easing the ferocity of his approach in villages that the hacendados, who

were concerned that no one would be left to work their plantations, vouched for—and kept the *Zapatistas* on the defensive. A political means to suppress the uprising was not entirely abandoned, however. General Leyva came to Cuernavaca on February 20 to negotiate with certain rebels, particularly de la O, but not, significantly, Zapata. At the beginning of March, Jacobo Ramos Martínez, who replaced Velázquez as lieutenant governor, sought avenues to negotiate with Zapata. The problem for Leyva and Ramos Martínez was Robles, whose actions had widened the division between rebels, as well as those who might have remained passive, and Madero's government. The option of negotiating a peace, an idea Madero also explored through forming a commission that was studying the underlying cause of unrest in Morelos, became increasingly less likely. The willingness of the *Zapatistas* to accept government offers was perhaps best summed up in a letter Zapata sent to de la O and Pedro Celestino on March 17. Zapata noted, "everything the government offers is a lie . . . you all take possession of the lands yourselves in accordance with the titles and maps of the pueblo, and in case the government does not recognize it, you settle it with weapons in hand."[7] About six weeks later, Madero's commission issued its report, which blamed the unrest on the agrarian problem, and urged the hacendados, who had insisted to the commission that the discontent of the campesinos stemmed from their ignorantly accepting propaganda spread by agitators, to "recognize the difficult situation the state is in . . . [and to] sacrific[e] whatever is necessary of the interests and prerogatives that they previously enjoyed."[8] In other words, the commission suggested that the hacendados give back to the villages the land that they had taken.

By the time that report was released, Zapata was even less likely to negotiate. At the end of March, the *Zapatistas* went on the offensive again, forcing Robles to confine his forces, some of which had been redeployed to the north where Orozco had launched his rebellion, to the larger towns. Despite establishing de facto control over the countryside, Zapata could not wrest control of the entire state from the government. The *Zapatistas* were constantly obliged to take strategic withdrawals. Zapata, for example, had taken Jonacatepec on April 2, and four days later, his forces attacked Jojutla, Tlaquiltenango, and Tlaltizapán, but they could not maintain a presence in them. In fact, their ability to hold onto territory weakened as their offensive became more relentless. By early May, the *Zapatistas* were suffering from shortages of ammunition. They had, at one point, unsuccessfully appealed to Orozco for arms, hoping they could be smuggled into the region over water and through Guerrero. The cost of success, in short, damaged the chances of achieving a complete victory. Another problem that led to a slackening of attacks was the need for recruits to return to their homes for the planting season. The result was a virtual stalemate between *Zapatistas* in the countryside and the *federales* in the towns.

Naranjo saw in the lull of attacks an opportunity. Telling Madero, with unwarranted optimism, that the *federales* would soon take control of the south, Naranjo pushed the president to remove Robles from Morelos and worked to guarantee that martial law would come to an end on May 19, as it was scheduled to do. On that day, an election having already been arranged by Naranjo, most places voted in an electoral college, which, the following week, elected reformers who had sought legal means to end the injustices in Morelos. They were not, however, sworn into office until July 12, the month after Robles was sent to Puebla and General Felipe Ángeles took control of the federal forces in the state. Ángeles proved a perfect complement to Naranjo. He understood that Robles's approach to suppressing rebellion was counterproductive. He thus put an end to the resettlement policy and did all he could to rebuild the life of the villages. He even refused to reintroduce harsh methods of suppression, despite his being urged to do so, after soldiers and civilians were killed during *Zapatista* attacks on trains near the end of July and at the beginning of August, a period in which the *Zapatistas* were able to stage almost daily attacks on either army outposts or trains. Ángeles was so confident that he refused to change his tactics even after his own wife was caught up in a *Zapatista* attack while travelling to Cuernavaca to be with him. Ángeles's goal was not to force Morelos into submission but to unite its cause to Madero's. "I would give anything," he told Mrs. King, "to show these people the mistake they are making. President Madero is doing his best for them, but he needs cooperation. The conservatives, using all the tricks of politics, fight him at every step, and how can he force through his reforms if the people he wants to help will not back him?"[9]

Ángeles's tactics had the desired effect: Zapata's men—those who had returned home to plant their villages' fields in the spring and those who found they could now go home without the threat of being attacked—realized they were able to live in peace and were content to wait for the legislature to enact reform. The rebellion in Morelos was in the process of being put to an end. In fact, only a small number of rebel groups, many of them actual bandits, continued to operate in the state by the summer's end. Ángeles was pleased, telling a reporter that "through his application of reason and justice . . . there was no revolution here in the South."[10] Zapata would remember this period as a time in which he feared his movement was genuinely threatened with defeat, although he did not act on such fears when offered another opportunity to make peace. Encouraged by the lack of *Zapatista* activities during the summer, Madero's government again reached out to Zapata. The new minister of the interior, Jesús Flores Magón—a former anarchist whom Zapata had sought out in 1909 for advice about opposing Díaz's regime—sent an envoy to Zapata's headquarters, with Madero's blessing. Zapata still distrusted Madero and refused to negotiate, telling the messenger, "The revolution in Morelos is not a local revolution. . . . Not until Madero's downfall will we enter into peace agreements."[11] Zapata and his chiefs, none of whom accepted the amnesty Naranjo offered them, bided their time, encouraged perhaps by rumors that disloyal government officials were plotting against Madero. They eventually threatened to put to death the messengers that Madero kept sending to push Zapata to agree to unacceptable peace terms.

In the meantime, the state legislature, which was composed primarily of ordinary, if respected, locals who accepted the principles of the revolution as Zapata understood them, was doing all it could to challenge the notion that rebellion was necessary, proposing legislation that would aid small landowners and small merchants. Its efforts would be halted by the truncated nature of its legislative session. The next election was to take place in August: those sworn into office in July had taken their seats at the end of the official term of the 22nd legislature, which had begun late because of the rebellion. The next legislature was to convene on September 16, leaving the 22nd legislature little time to do anything but appoint Aniceto Villamar—a local Tepoztlán lawyer and, therefore, a more acceptable leader than Naranjo, despite the latter's progressive policies, to the people—as the new interim governor. He began his stint in office by promising to acknowledge the rights of campesinos who had been dispossessed of their land and praising Zapata's efforts in the state during the *Maderista* revolution. Soon afterward, things became so bad for the *Zapatistas* that many villages stopped offering them safe havens. Zapata spent much of the fall of 1912 traveling from one safe house to another in Guerrero, Puebla, and eastern Morelos, the area of his home state that had served as his base of operations for most of the year.

The new legislature contained almost no members of the 22nd one, most of them having chosen not to run for reelection on the principle that reform meant an end to allowing the same group of men to hold continual power. It moved slowly on reform, failing to vote and undermining the progress that its predecessor had made. Rather than voting on the legislation proposed over the summer, the new legislature spent its time in debate about the possibility of reform, and the few times that reform measures did come to a vote, they were defeated. Quickly passing reforms into law would prevent their consequences from being properly studied, it was argued, and it was decided that social problems needed to be resolved over time or that chaos would result. The legislature then turned to what its members felt was the more pressing matter of suppressing rebellion, even though the *Zapatista* movement was in decline before it refused to enact any kind of reform.

Denouncing the central government's contention that Morelos would soon be pacified, the legislature insisted that the state's security concerns urgently needed to be addressed. In October and November, it began pushing the central government to strengthen the garrisons in the region. The work that had been taking place to convince rebels to put down their arms was also stopped, partially because the state's legislators' raised concerns about the possibility of such work succeeding and objected to the bribes that those doing it were giving to midlevel officers to stop them from fighting. Of course, the alarms were not completely inaccurate, especially during November and afterwards. As the push toward reform stopped, some of the peasantry again looked to Zapata for solutions, and recruits slowly returned to his army. He soon began to lay the groundwork for resuming his revolutionary activities, holding a junta on November 1 to decide how to move forward. The issue under discussion was financing, and Zapata and his chiefs arrived at a solution to the problem that would enable them to pay for their activities without relying on the villages, a practice that risked alienating their primary supporters. They would levy a tax on the hacendados; those who refused to pay would have their sugarcane fields burned.

Many haciendas did refuse to pay the tax, and their fields were burned. Others paid it, providing much needed funds to the *Zapatistas*, and putting themselves under threat from government reprisals. Escandón, who had returned to the state after Madero proved victorious, even went to jail. Recruitment for the rebel forces continued to rise, in part because the haciendas on which fields had been burned could provide no work. Full-scale rebellion, however, would not resume immediately. The harvest, after all, had been good in 1912, and many in the villages seemed content to wait and see whether their politicians would work out the issues that were slowing down land reform. Two political events suggested that such a wait-and-see attitude was appropriate. First, the swearing in of Patricio Leyva as the first post-

Full-length formal portrait of Emiliano Zapata in military regalia. (Library of Congress, Prints and Photographs Division, LC-DIG-ggbain-14906) (Library of Congress)

revolutionary elected governor on December 1 was an encouraging sign. Leyva, after all, had been elected, not appointed, and had been, at least according to his campaign rhetoric, on the side of the peasants in 1909. Leyva's election, in any case, brought an air of legitimacy to the state's government. Another positive sign was that the legislature was set to pass a bill that was written to satisfy the recommendations of Madero's commission earlier in the year and that would have restored, at least partially, the rights the villages had to communal lands and resources. Leyva, however, vetoed the bill, arguing that the legislature had overstepped its constitutional power, having no right to pass legislation that concerned communal property. A few days later, on December 13, a bill was introduced to reduce the taxes of those who had suffered financially, in other words the hacendados, during the *Maderista* uprising in 1911. That measure passed and was signed into law.

The campesinos now lost any faith they had in the government, and they again turned to Zapata, the only figure willing to fight for their interests, and the rate of recruitment for the *Zapatistas* rapidly increased.[12] The major towns, nevertheless, were well protected, and the politicians, as well as the wealthy, felt secure, confident that they had years to study the social problems plaguing their state and to find solutions that would not disrupt the order of things. The *Zapatistas* further consolidated their hold over Morelos's countryside throughout December and January, but they lacked the ability to assert their influence where it most mattered, the center of Morelos's power, Cuernavaca. That city was protected by the power of the central government, which despite its own problems in imposing itself on Mexico as a whole, was concerned enough with the problem of *Zapatismo* to defend its allies in Morelos. Madero's presidency, however, would not last much longer: revolutionary Mexico would soon be pulled in another direction.

NOTES

1. Some sources—for example, Philip S. Jowett, A. M. De Quesada, and Stephen Walsh, *The Mexican Revolution, 1910–20* (New York: Osprey, 2006), 47—date the emergence of this command structure at the beginning of 1912, perhaps at the suggestion of Roger Parkinson, who notes that it was in place by 1912 in his *Zapata: A Biography* (Briarcliff

Manor, NY: Stein & Day, 1980 [1975]), 122. John H. McNeely, by contrast, suggests the command structure was in place for the signing of the Plan de Ayala, though the number of colonels was 17 when that happened. See his "Origins of the Zapata Revolt in Morelos," *Hispanic American Historical Review* 46, no. 2 (May 1966), 165.

2. Quoted in John Womack, *Zapata and the Mexican Revolution* (New York: Vintage Books, 1970 [1968]), 131.

3. Quoted in Adolfo Gilly, *The Mexican Revolution*, trans. Patrick Camiller (New York: New Press, 2005 [1971]), 75.

4. Quoted in Frank McLynn, *Villa and Zapata: A History of the Mexican Revolution* (New York: Carroll & Graf, 2002), 121.

5. Quoted Womack, *Zapata and the Mexican Revolution*, 136.

6. Quoted in McLynn, *Villa and Zapata*, 122.

7. Quoted in Paul Hart, *Bitter Harvest* (Albuquerque: University of New Mexico Press, 2005), 211.

8. Ibid., 210–11.

9. Quoted in Rosa E. King, *Tempest over Mexico: A Personal Chronicle* (New York: Little Brown, 1940 [1935]), 99. For an account of Ángeles's wife's encounter with the *Zapatistas*, see pages 100–101.

10. Quoted in Womack, *Zapata and the Mexican Revolution*, 151.

11. Quoted in Parkinson, *Zapata: A Biography*, 139.

12. Despite the increase in recruitment, Harry H. Dunn is either exaggerating or mistaking the numbers with estimates from a year later, when he claims that there were, "as 1912 became 13 . . . , twenty thousand or more Zapatistas, well mounted, well armed [and abundantly munitioned]." See *The Crimson Jester: Zapata of Mexico* (New York: R. M. McBride, 1934), 179.

Chapter 6

THE RISE AND FALL
OF HUERTA

The south had not been the only region in which Madero faced problems in 1912. Rebellion also broke out in the north, particularly in Chihuahua. Pascual Orozco became the leader of that uprising, which was connected for a short time to Emilio Vásquez Gómez, whose opposition to the direction the revolution had been taking had been growing since his dismissal from de la Barra's interim government. Vásquez Gómez, however, was in the United States when his followers, some of whom referred to themselves as *Zapatistas* rather than *Vasquistas*, broke into open revolt at the end of February. That revolt forced Orozco to break fully with Madero, who was at that stage offering Orozco the governorship of Chihuahua. Many of those who had taken up arms as *Vasquistas* trusted Orozco—who was ordered, in his capacity as the commander of the state's *rurales*, to stamp out the new revolt—more than they trusted their leader. They gave him the option of joining them or losing their trust, which would have hindered his ability to rebel later on. The man whom Zapata had named "the illustrious General Pascual Orozco" in the Plan de Ayala thus returned to revolutionary activities because circumstances had forced his hand. At first, he seemed ready to become a

Vasquista, although he assumed leadership of the movement within a matter of weeks after joining it.[1]

The revolt in Chihuahua was a positive development for Zapata but not because Orozco took the place Zapata had offered him as head of the Liberating Army. Indeed, Orozco never provided help to the rebels in Morelos, failing even to reply to Zapata's request for arms in April. Problems in the north led to panic in Mexico City, especially after General José Salas, who gave up his position as minister of war to take charge of the forces that were sent to confront Orozco, was beaten. He was wounded on the battlefield almost as soon as he arrived in Chihuahua and ordered to retreat by Madero. Shortly thereafter, he committed suicide. Madero, much against his better judgment but at the insistence of his cabinet, was obliged to recall General Huerta from retirement, who returned to duty on March 12, 1912. He promised Madero, "I'll whip him [Orozco]. I guarantee it,"[2] as he headed north to take command. During this period, troops were removed from Morelos, spreading Robles's forces thin. It was in this context that the *Zapatistas* were able to retake the initiative: Zapata's ability to undermine Robles's policy of terror had been made possible, at least in part, by the northern uprising.

The bigger issue for Madero, although he could not completely know it at the time, was Huerta. In the summer of 1912, the general was an asset to the government. He was able, after all, to put a stop to Orozco's rebellion by the end of July, even though Orozco remained at large and fought on. On September 12, he fled to the United States, where he tried unsuccessfully to keep his forces together from afar. But there were problems with putting so much faith in Huerta. He and Madero disliked each other. Madero also seemed to distrust Huerta and worried about the consequences of alienating him, something evidenced by Madero's keeping Pancho Villa, whom Huerta detested and wanted to get rid of, in prison for months without adequate cause. Madero had good reason to be concerned. Huerta had reportedly told his officers, "If I wanted to, I could make an agreement with Pascual Orozco and I would go to Mexico City with twenty-seven thousand men and take the presidency away from Madero."[3] Madero, at first, downplayed the threat such statements suggested, promoting Huerta a short time after becoming aware of the insubordinate remarks to major general.

In October, however, Madero began to take seriously the danger Huerta posed and removed him from his command.[4]

Another crisis then emerged. Porfirio Díaz's nephew, Felix Díaz, staged his own rebellion in Veracruz, a major Mexican port, persuading army units in the region to join him and return honor to the region. This uprising, which began on October 16, lasted only a few days, and Díaz, after the Supreme Court ruled that the death sentence handed down by a military court was unconstitutional, was sent to the same prison, a military facility at Santiago Tlatelolco, that housed Reyes, who had staged his own disastrous revolt in the last months of 1911. From prison, Reyes and Díaz became involved in a plot to oust Madero that was being orchestrated among 22 generals with the help of Henry Lane Wilson, the U.S. ambassador to Mexico, who had developed a fanatical hatred of Madero and saw the present plot as the last chance to see him removed from office—Lane Wilson knew he would be recalled from his post once the incoming U.S. president, Woodrow Wilson, was sworn into office in March. Unaware of the discontent of the generals, Madero was feeling, as the historian Frank McLynn observes, "more confident than at any time in his presidency. He had defeated Orozco, vanquished Felix Díaz and humbled Huerta."[5] Such confidence apparently led Madero to ignore his brother Gustavo's revelation of the existence of the new plot, along with the list of generals involved in it, on February 4, 1913. Indeed, Madero treated the news as a fiction, particularly because Huerta was described as a possible participant rather than as the leader. Madero did not believe Huerta would take any role other than the principal one.

Huerta held back his support because the position that he was offered was below that of the president, which Reyes was to become on an interim basis. Díaz was to be elected to give constitutional authority to the new government. Huerta only got on board once the shooting began, although exactly when he altered his position is a matter of speculation. On the day the coup began, February 9, General Manuel Mondragón freed Díaz and Reyes from prison, and Reyes headed to the National Palace to declare himself president. He was met by gunfire and killed. In the same battle, Madero's General Lauro Villar was seriously wound, and Huerta, who met Madero as he headed toward the National Palace and offered his help, took control of the government's forces. Over the next 10 days, an episode referred to as *Decena Tragica* (the Tragic Ten), Díaz's forces and Huerta's exchanged fire, seemingly battling each other during the first days. But it soon became apparent to close observers that the opposing forces were avoiding engaging one another as much as possible, firing only at less strategic enemy targets—although Huerta is said to have order those most loyal to Madero to go on suicide missions. Díaz and Huerta had entered into an agreement, and on February 17, Gustavo unearthed Huerta's deception and arrested the general, whom Madero released and returned to his command. Over the next 24 hours, Huerta had both Madero and his brother arrested. Gustavo was killed soon afterward. In the meantime, Huerta announced that he was going to assume the presidency, and with the help of Lane Wilson, who had, some historians believe, served as the go between for Huerta and Díaz during the Tragic Ten, bullied Díaz into accepting the idea.

Huerta was sworn into office on February 19. Three days later, while Madero and his vice president, Pino Suárez, were being transferred from the National Palace to a Mexico City prison, their car was attacked, and Madero and Suárez were killed, having been shot while trying to escape, at least according to the official version of events, which reads:

Madero and Pino Suárez, who have been detained at the Palace at the disposition of the War Department, were taken to the penitentiary in accordance with a previous decision, as the result of which the same was placed yesterday afternoon under the charge of an army officer for its better security.

When the automobiles had traversed about two-thirds of the way to the penitentiary, however, they were attacked by an armed group, and the escorts descended from the machines to offer resistance. Suddenly the group grew larger, and the prisoners tried to escape.

An exchange of shots then took place, in which two of the attacking party were killed and two wounded. Both prisoners were killed. The automobiles were badly damaged.

The President and his Cabinet have resolved that the affair shall be consigned to the military judicial authorities, having to do with the attempts against military prisoners, such as were Madero and Pino Suárez, so that they may make a strict investigation with the direct intervention of the Military Prosecutor General.

The Government promises that society shall be fully satisfied as to the facts in the case. The commanders of the escort are now under arrest, and the facts above recorded have been ascertained so as to clear up this unhappy event, however incomprehensible it may be under the present sad circumstances.[6]

The facts in the case were never determined to the satisfaction of anyone, as the circumstances of the attack were not investigated. Historians assume that Huerta had Madero killed, as the new president had the most to gain from getting rid of the man he overthrew. "Mexico has been saved! From now on we shall have peace, progress, and prosperity," Lane Wilson told the diplomatic core in Mexico and, in a written statement to the State Department in Washington, observed, "A wicked despotism has fallen!"[7] Concerned with U.S. financial interests, he believed Huerta could put a stop to the banditry of such figures as Zapata and secure U.S. investments in the region by unifying the country behind a strong central government similar to Porfirio Díaz's.

Unity was what the new government set out to achieve. Huerta, along with Felix Díaz, signed a statement that called for all revolutionary movements to unite behind the federal army shortly after Madero's arrest,[8] and while some heeded that call (Orozco, for example), others (including Zapata) would not. During the Tragic Ten, Zapata had taken advantage of Madero's withdrawing General Ángeles and his troops from Morelos, and the *Zapatistas* were quickly mobilized into occupying forces in Cuautla, Yautepec, and Jonacatepec. Zapata was intent on seizing on the opportunity that had been handed to him. Huerta, likely doubtful of his ability to make peace with Zapata, soon began sending peace envoys to other *Zapatista* leaders—for example Jesús "One-Eyed" Morales, who did accept terms with the new government—in an attempt to weaken the movement. Zapata wasn't completely ignored. He was approached by a number of envoys, the most significant of which seems to have been the father of Orozco. Orozco, Sr., actually managed to get Zapata to suggest he would attend talks so long as the *federales* that were still in Morelos were withdrawn. He had no intention of making peace with Huerta. The demand was a trick, and Zapata ordered his troops to attack the *federales* as they withdrew.

Huerta's apparent concessions may also have been part of an elaborate trick to get Zapata to make himself vulnerable and then have him assassinated. Whatever Huerta's intentions were, he was skeptical of his chances of coming to an agreement, telling the U.S. ambassador, "The best means to handle the rebel chiefs [in Morelos] is an 18 cents rope wherefrom to hang them."[9] He also placed two enemies of the *Zapatistas* in prominent positions, making de la Barra, who had been serving as an opposition senator during Madero's presidency, vice president and returning Alberto García Granados to the position of minister of the interior. Indeed, holding a moderate position in Huerta's Mexico became increasingly impossible, and those reformists in Morelos who had been too conservative for the *Zapatistas* came to feel that their positions were precarious. Leyva, for example, resigned as governor, taking a safer position as a member of the state legislature.

Meanwhile, Zapata began to put Huerta's peace envoys on trial for treason, a move that was meant to demonstrate not simply his disdain for Huerta's offers of peace but also his desire to adhere, if only for show in the present circumstances, to a legitimate system of justice, one that sought the opinion of a court before carrying out executions. The judge was Montaño, and the prosecutor was Manuel Palafox, a Puebla-born former engineering student who had worked as a salesman and accountant throughout Mexico. He had initially arrived in Zapata's camp in October 1911 with the offer of a bribe from his then-employer the Tenango hacienda. Instead of shooting him, Zapata held him prisoner until someone was needed for a diplomatic mission in San Antonio. Upon his return, Palafox's managerial skills proved increasingly useful, and by 1913, he had set about professionalizing the *Zapatista* organization. His service as a prosecutor would consolidate his importance to Zapata. Along with Antonio Díaz Soto y Gama, a socialist intellectual who fled Mexico City when Huerta took power, Palafox would come to rank among the most important intellectual *Zapatista* figures, while Montaño's prestige went into decline.

The treason trials had served, in part, as hype. During March and April, Zapata stepped up his propaganda campaign, sending open letters to Díaz and Orozco, among others, in which he explained the need for the revolution to go on even though Madero was gone. Zapata also condemned Orozco for surrendering the principles for which the peasantry had fought and died. Orozco's putting down arms was particularly troublesome, as it provided Huerta with an example to parade before those with whom his government was negotiating. That example was what convinced Jesús "One-Eyed" Morales, among others, to retire from revolutionary activities. Through these months, the fighting continued, and the now typical stalemate in which the *federales* controlled the major towns and the *Zapatistas* controlled the countryside was reestablished. The *Zapatistas* went on attacking the railways, but the *federales* slackened the pressure it put on them. Huerta was focusing his army's resources on the north and held off sending as many troops as he thought would be needed in Morelos until April, when General Robles returned.

Robles quickly reestablished a campaign along the lines of his previous one, but this time he took control not just of the military in the region but of the civil government as well. The new approach, as Huerta proclaimed in a speech to Morelos' land owners at the end of April, would follow "extreme measures, for the government is going, so to speak, to depopulate the state, and will send your haciendas other workers,"[10] which was the only way, he explained, to clear the state of *Zapatistas*, whom he, as Robles had done before him, defined as the entire rural population. "*Zapatismo* will be exterminated, cost what it may," he assured Mexico City the following month,[11] and those who would pay, it now became clear, were the people of Morelos. Depopulation programs would soon be carried out in regions throughout Mexico, the idea apparently being to pacify the people by relocating them, and the cruelty of Huerta's Mexico came to be regarded as ordinary. "Dainty women talked unconcernedly about *peons* hung on telegraph poles and the 'funny way' in which soldiers spun round when they were shot. Genial Britons and Americans spoke of the execution of prisoners as a regular practice and approved it, because 'if the Mexicans would only exterminate one another, the country would have a chance,'" the reporter H. Hamilton Fyfe observed.[12]

Zapata had stepped up his campaign before Huerta had laid out his plans, attacking Jonacatapec, where his victorious forces seized valuable weapons as well as General Higinio Aguilar and 47 other officers, whom Zapata went on to pardon, after securing their promise to stop fighting the rebellion. Aguilar not only kept that promise but joined the *Zapatistas*, providing them with military expertise and useful contacts that enabled them to buy weapons from *federales* more concerned with turning a profit than with who won the war. Zapata went on to lay siege to Cuautla before April ended, and his forces subjected the Cuernavaca area to continual attacks in the first weeks of May. Robles's campaign had now started in earnest: everyone living in rural villages was required to settle in camps near larger towns or face execution without trial, and hundreds of rural people were soon sent to Mexico City to provide recruits for the *federales* in their fight against Venustiano Carranza, a Porfirian governor who now aligned himself with the revolution, and Pancho Villa, the other powerful opposition leader in the north. "I am trying to clean up your beautiful Morelos for you," Robles explained to King. "What a nice place it will be once we get rid of the *Morelenses!* If they resist me, I shall hang them like earrings to the trees."[13]

Robles was incapable of carrying out his promise, and trying to do so was counterproductive. The rural people, who were better acquainted with the region, were often able to hide when the *federales* showed up in their villages and return later on, when it was safe to do so. Left with no other option, they would then join the *Zapatistas*. As a man remembering the period years later explained to Rosa King, "the Federals, in the name of the Revolutionary government, had come unexpectedly upon the little piece of ground his father owned, and had shot his father dead before his eyes and his mother's, and then set fire to their poor hut, all to steal the corn they had planted. He and his mother fled, hiding in the fields and woods, anywhere for safety, until they could find Emiliano Zapata, the protector and avenger. The boy was only fifteen at the time, but his father lay dead and his home was in ruins. The *Zapatistas* gave him a gun. 'With my gun in hand and hatred in my heart, I killed and destroyed wherever I could.'"[14] Even Robles's successes helped to swell Zapata's army, for among the new recruits were women, who "formed their own battalion and revolted 'to avenge the dead,'"[15] that is, the men who were killed in battle or by execution or who had been deported.

The idea of "cost what it may" was also proving unpalatable to the hacendados, who were losing their workers either to the draft or the

Zapatistas and who were alarmed because they were finding it difficult to run their operations. Robles, they feared, would destroy them in the process of crushing the *Zapatistas*. Meanwhile, Huerta's attempt to force such regions in central and southern Mexico as Michoacán, Guerrero, Mexico State, Tlaxcala, Puebla, the Federal District, Oaxaca, Hidalgo, Veracruz, San Luis Potosí, Durango, and even Chihuahua in the north to submit to his rule was creating allies for Zapata. Rebel leaders throughout the country, most importantly Pancho Villa, declared their allegiance to the Plan de Ayala. The support, while welcomed, raised the problem of managing a loose confederation of forces, the leaders of which were not in contact with each other or with Zapata. To alleviate the difficulty, Zapata issued a revised Plan de Ayala on May 30. It declared Huerta a usurper, denounced Orozco as unworthy of the honor the previous version of the plan had bestowed upon him, and made Zapata the official chief of the movement. The revision was followed in June with instructions about the treatment of troops, who were to be paid or helped in other ways, and occupied villages. These instructions also contained rules about carrying out agrarian reform, specifically provision six of the Plan de Ayala, which proclaimed that "the pueblos or citizens who have the titles corresponding to those properties will immediately enter into possession of that real estate of which they have been despoiled by the bad faith of our oppressors."[16] Field officers would now be allowed to aid in the process of reappropriating land, whereas before, it was suggested, only *Zapatista* leaders in Morelos could do so.

These instructions were not followed uniformly, and violence was committed against *pacíficos* in villages, something Zapata had always denounced, even by *Zapatistas* in Morelos. Yet Zapata continued to garner respect among the people: "all through the South, they love him loyally/ for he gives them justice, Peace, Progress, and Liberty," one folk song proclaimed.[17] The southern revolution was now becoming *Zapatista* in earnest, and Robles responded by intensifying his efforts, still confident in his ability to stamp out the movement. He would soon assert that rebellion would be completely crushed by an attack on Huautla, where Zapata had set up a temporary headquarters, in August. Having advanced notice of the plans, which Robles had bragged about to the press, Zapata evacuated his forces from the area before the battle began. Thus Robles's forces took control of an empty settlement, finding only the bodies of peace envoys who had been executed as traitors. Robles, nonetheless, declared victory and was promoted to divisional general. The whole episode was a farce. The *Zapatistas* continued to control the countryside, and the *federales* were unable to do anything but hold onto the large towns that had been recaptured back in March, before Robles arrived.

In June, Huerta was obliged to withdraw troops from the south to fight rebels in the north. In Morelos, Robles was replaced with Brigadier General Adolfo Jiménez Castro, who did little more than maintain the status quo. Although Zapata was unable to defeat the *federales* where they were garrisoned, he did not sit still. In September, he moved his headquarters into northern Guerrero and began preparations for a major offensive in the hope of forcing Huerta to postpone the elections that he had promised to hold in October, elections that might risk giving legitimacy to the new government, which Huerta had promised not to lead. The position the rebels might attain if they could defeat a federal government that had been accepted by world leaders would be weakened. The task was a daunting one, requiring Zapata to forge the forces of various allies into a single army. He began by issuing new instructions to the Liberating Army of the Center and South, as it was now being called, in order to further professionalize it. *Corporal* and *sergeant* were added to the list of officers, and soldiers were now required to follow orders of all higher-ranking officers, regardless of whether the officer belonged to the company in which particular soldiers fought or not. Desertion became a punishable offence, making joining the *Zapatistas* akin to joining the actual army. On the positive side, soldiers were given assurances that they would be paid for their services. Zapata also kept his eye on retaining the hearts of the people, making stricter rules against abusing the population.

Zapata hoped these changes, specifically the one requiring soldiers to follow the orders of all officers, would allow the *Zapatistas* to quickly mobilize a large force for the major offensive that Zapata planned to pull off to prevent the rapidly approaching election. Other events would make such an offensive unnecessary in the immediate future. Burgeoning congressional opposition to Huerta, which threatened, on October 9, to put its support behind the Constitutionalists, as the northern rebels were called, in protest of the murder of the senator

Belisario Domínguez, led Huerta to dissolve Congress and take complete control of the government. The election still proceeded, and Huerta, making a move that has come to be known as "Huerta's second coup,"[18] declared himself a candidate and was elected president by a wide majority, while the new Congress was filled with his supporters. Huerta would not defend the legitimacy of the election, the element that Zapata feared could threaten the momentum of Zapatismo, when the courts declared it invalid, and he felt obliged to call for a new election in July 1913 but not to step down from his position. This episode gave Zapata more time for organizing his resistance on a large scale, and before the elections were held, he published a manifesto that declared that the Zapatistas were close to victory.

Zapata's confidence stemmed, in part, from his ability to see the difficulties that Huerta was creating for himself on the international stage. Zapata thus reached out to Washington, whose refusal to recognize Huerta's legitimacy was now sure to continue, for a loan. He also tried to join his movement with that in the north. These efforts bore no fruit, but Zapata did strengthen his southern alliances during this time. A number of chiefs in Guerrero formally submitted to Zapata's authority, among them Julián Blanco, who had fought the Zapatistas as a Maderista and become a Constitutionalist after Madero's fall. He signed a treaty confirming his acceptance of the Plan de Ayala in January 1914. Zapata had now amassed a truly impressive force but still lacked the weapons and ammunition that would be needed to fulfill his objective, which in the immediate future was to take Chilpancingo, Guerrera's state capital, and Zapata sometimes went to extreme lengths to acquire military supplies.

Throughout February, Zapatistas in Morelos distracted the federales with raids on district seats, sometimes staging as many as four in a single day, while those in Guerrero managed to occupy a number of towns in the northern part of the state. Huerta was powerless to stop the Zapatistas' momentum because problems in the north prevented him from sending reinforcements south, and on March 9, the Zapatistas began to build up forces around Chilpancingo. Troops led by Blanco took up positions to the city's south, while Jesús Salgado, who was in charge of the attack, stood to the west, and Heliodoro Castillo's forces lay to the north. Zapata arrived with about 2,000 reinforcements three days later, establishing a temporary headquarters in Tixtla, and on March 15, the siege began. A mutiny of soldiers in Jojutla occupied the army elsewhere and the *federales* in Chilpancingo, who were outnumbered by more than three to one, were left to defend themselves. A little more than a week later, the revolutionaries took control of the city, and the *federales* fled under the direction of General Luis Cartón. They were soon captured, and Cartón and the other officers were brought before Zapata in Tixla. The soldiers, some of whom joined the *Zapatistas*, were allowed to go free. The officers were court martialed, and many were executed, including Cartón, who faced a firing squad in Chilpancingo on October 6.

In the meantime, Salgado—in compliance with the 13th article of the Plan de Ayala—was appointed the state's provisional governor, but he continued to lead troops in the *Zapatista* offensive, taking Taxco and Buenavista de Cuéllar. By the time these victories were achieved, Zapata was back in Morelos, bringing with him weapons that had been captured in Chilpancingo and from those who had fled, and his forces were in control of the majority of Morelos, although the main centers of power remained in the hands of the *federales* in April. As usual, the difficulty of obtaining supplies, specifically ammunition, slowed down the *Zapatistas*, and they would have been unable to achieve more gains if the United States had not sent forces to Veracruz. The conflict with the Americans, who were stationed in the region to protect U.S. oil interests, began on April 9. Federal soldiers arrested a landing party from a U.S. warship in the port of Tampico. Although the men were released and the U.S. commander, Admiral Henry Mayo, was offered a robust apology, Mayo pushed the diplomatic envelope, making demands meant to embarrass the Mexican army. Huerta refused to comply, and on April 21, U.S. forces landed in Veracruz, taking control of the port after about 24 hours of fighting. Huerta hoped to use the incident to unite the various factions behind his authority, appealing to Carranza, Villa, and Zapata to help repel the invaders, but none offered help under the conditions that were offered.

Zapata was vehemently opposed to the U.S. intervention, telling his own chiefs that he would fight them if they invaded Morelos, but otherwise, he took advantage of the distraction they created for Huerta, who took troops out of Morelos to meet the crisis. The *Zapatistas* immediately took Jonacatepec, Cuautla, Yautepec, and Tetecala, four district seats, leaving only Jojutla and Cuernavaca in the hands of the *federales*, the former of which fell in early May and the latter of which, while not occupied, was placed under siege in June. By that time, Zapata had set his sights on taking Mexico City, apparently having determined that getting the agrarian reforms he wanted would require him to be directly involved in bringing down the government. Throughout June and into July, the *Zapatistas* advanced toward the capital, resisting the temptation to negotiate with the government even for the chance to get its members appointed to leading positions within it. Their distrust of the value of the offers was well grounded, for Huerta merely wanted to quiet the southern front to focus his resources in the north.

As the *Zapatistas* advanced from the south, the *Carrancistas* and *Villistas* advanced from the north, and with no chance of defeating the onslaught of revolutionaries, Huerta resigned on July 15, 1914, and went into exile. His government sought to fight on, appointing Francisco Carbajal as the interim president. The rebels refused to accept his authority, and Zapata continued to prepare to occupy Mexico City. "It is good to repeat that we will carry out no transactions with any government if it does not turn over the Supreme National Powers to the Revolution, without qualifications of any kind," he told his chiefs,[19] and published, on July 19, an Act of Ratification of the Plan de Ayala, in which he noted that the *Zapatistas'* goal was "before anything else the economic improvement of the great majority of Mexicans" and that they were opposed to "the infamous pretension of reducing everything to a simple change in the personnel of government."[20] They would only accept the authority of a government that integrated the Plan de Ayala into the country's constitution and removed from its ranks all agents of the previous regimes.

Zapata's refusal to negotiate with Carbajal's agents, who even promised to help bring legitimacy to the Plan de Ayala, and resolve to move his forces into the capital without making compromises would undermine the *Zapatistas'* position in the end. As the Constitutionalists, or the northern revolutionary forces, closed in on Mexico City, they agreed to meet with representatives of Carbajal's government, and officials from the War Department surrendered to Álvaro Obregón, a Constitutionalist general, on August 13. Zapata found himself, both literally and figuratively, left on the margins. His forces were holed up in the mountains to the south of Mexico City, unable to enter it because the federal troops that protected the path to it from the south held their positions, as the treaty that was signed stipulated they do, until they were replaced by Constitutionalist troops. Zapata's ability to impose his agenda or even to have its concerns addressed by the incoming regime was being denied, despite the importance of the *Zapatistas* in bringing down Huerta.

NOTES

1. See Friedrich Katz, *The Life and Times of Pancho Villa* (Stanford, CA: Stanford University Press, 1998), 139–40.

2. Quoted in Roger Parkinson, *Zapata: A Biography* (Briarcliff Manor, NY: Stein & Day, 1980 [1975]), 133.

3. Quoted in Enrique Krauze, *Mexico: Biography of Power; A History of Modern Mexico, 1810–1996*, trans. Hank Heifetz (New York: HarperCollins, 1998), 265.

4. See Katz, *Life and Times of Pancho Villa*, 178.

5. Frank McLynn, *Villa and Zapata: A History of the Mexican Revolution* (New York: Carroll & Graf, 2002), 145.

6. Frederick Starr, *Mexico and the United States: A Story of Revolution, Intervention and War* (Chicago: The Bible House, 1914), 379, 381.

7. Quoted in Lesley Byrd Simpson, *Many Mexicos* (Berkeley: University of California Press, 1967 [1962]), 300.

8. See Parkinson, *Zapata: A Biography*, 148.

9. Quoted in Michael J. Gonzales, *The Mexican Revolution, 1910–1940* (Albuquerque: University of New Mexico Press, 2002), 131.

10. Quoted in John Womack, *Zapata and the Mexican Revolution* (New York: Vintage Books, 1970 [1968]), 165.

11. Quoted in Samuel Brunk, *The Posthumous Career of Emiliano Zapata* (Austin: University of Texas Press, 2008), 95.

12. H. Hamilton Fyfe, *The Real Mexico* (New York: McBride, Nast, 1914), 4.

13. Quoted in Rosa King, *Tempest over Mexico: A Personal Chronicle* (New York: Little Brown, 1940 [1935]), 93.

14. Ibid., 89.

15. Gonzales, *Mexican Revolution*, 131.

16. Plan de Ayala, trans. John Womack, http://www.hist.umn.edu/~rmccaa/la20c/ayala.htm.

17. Quoted in Womack, *Zapata and the Mexican Revolution*, 173.

18. John S. D. Eisenhower, *Intervention! The United States and the Mexican Revolution, 1913–1917* (New York: W. W. Norton, 1993), 61.

19. Quoted in Womack, *Zapata and the Mexican Revolution*, 188.

20. Ibid.

Chapter 7

THE REVOLUTION ENTERS
A NEW PHASE

The *Zapatistas* may have been isolated from the revolutionary victors by the deal that put an official end to the *Huerista* government, but the Constitutionalists could not simply ignore Zapata. Although they kept the *Zapatistas* out of Mexico City, the *Zapatistas* kept them out of the parts of the Federal District to the south of the capital. Forming a government with authority over the entire country could hardly have seemed realistic without the cooperation of Zapata, but dealing with him was complicated by a number of factors. Chief among them was the mutual distrust between Zapata and Carranza. The division within the Constitutionalist movement between the Carranza faction, which had taken control of Mexico City and allowed Carranza to assume the position of First Chief of Mexico on August 20, and the one led by Villa would also create difficulties. Zapata, after all, had already written to Villa earlier in the year and saw in him something of a natural ally,[1] so if Villa and Zapata joined forces, the power of the *Carrancistas* would be threatened.

Carranza needed to recognize the importance of preventing an alliance between Zapata and Villa from forming if he were to succeed in becoming Mexico's leader. At first, however, he seems to have underestimated the threat represented by Zapata, whom he always regarded, even after Zapata's real strength became obvious, as little more than "rabble."[2] In fact, Carranza resisted his generals' suggestion that he reach out to Zapata, even as those generals were beginning to do so themselves. Carranza's skepticism concerning the value of negotiating, once he finally accepted the wisdom of doing so, is made clear by his attitude toward land reform, the primary issue for the *Zapatistas*: "This land-redistribution business is absurd," he is reported to have said to an agent of de la O. "Tell me which haciendas you own and are able to redistribute, so that each of you can redistribute what belongs to you and not to someone else."[3] Carranza's attitude not only illustrates how far apart the two sides were but also suggests that his agreeing to talk with the *Zapatistas* was little more than a diversionary tactic. Indeed, in the spring, he had written to Francisco Vásquez Gómez, Emilio Vásquez Gómez's brother, and explained that he was only willing to talk with those who agree to adhere "unconditionally to the Plan of Guadalupe, without any compromise on the part of the Constitutionalist movement which I head."[4] Zapata seemed equally stubborn, having recently published another manifesto, one that reiterated his position that the Plan de Ayala must be adopted without change,[5] while calling for the revolutionary leaders to join together, appoint an interim president, and accept the Plan de Ayala. If they refused, the manifesto warned, the *Zapatistas* were prepared to fight on.

Despite the inflexibility of his rhetoric, Zapata did express a willingness to meet with Carranza in Yautepec, but Carranza would not travel to Morelos, insisting that any meeting would have to take place in Mexico City, where Zapata refused to go. The chances that the *Zapatistas* would unite with the larger national revolution seemed increasingly unlikely and continued to seem that way even after Carranza allowed envoys to travel to Cuernavaca, where Zapata had established his headquarters after the fall of the Huerta regime. The principal envoys were Antonio I. Villarreal and Luis Cabrera, whom Zapata had contacted in the belief that their revolutionary principles demonstrated that they were more likely to accept the Plan de Ayala. A third figure, Lucio Blanco, the general in charge of the *Carrancistas* involved in the standoff with the *Zapatistas* south of Mexico City, was not permitted to join the other two. This was probably because Carranza regarded him as more liberal than the others and feared he might unwittingly agree to things Carranza had no intention of accepting. Whatever his exact reasoning for disallowing Blanco's participation, Carranza had not sent Villarreal and Cabrera to negotiate a compromise to unify the revolution, having forbidden them to make any concessions whatsoever.

The situation in Cuernavaca also did not suggest that a spirit of compromise was in the air. The problem had very little to do with the fact that Zapata had written to Villarreal and Cabrera, as well as to Villa separately, in the hope of stirring up disagreement among the Constitutionalists so that Carranza could be replaced by a more acceptable figure, nor did it involve conflict among the *Zapatistas*, though such conflict did exist. The *Zapatista* officers, for example, had appointed de la O as the provisional governor, despite Zapata's favoring Francisco Pacheco, a chief whose base of operations was close to de la O's and who had been at odds with de la O almost since the latter had joined the *Zapatistas*. Another issue that created conflict was how the *Zapatistas* should deal with the Constitutionalists. Ángel Barrio, a former *Maderista* who had turned against Madero and was among the intellectuals who fled to Morelos when Huerta became president, had been working to unify the two movements, and he consequently came into conflict with Palafox, whom he accused of undermining his efforts, warning Zapata that Palafox's insistence on not compromising "will occasion grave evils for the revolution."[6] Such problems were under the surface. What Villarreal and Cabrera saw was an egalitarian democracy in which the educated and the uneducated were working together to find solutions to the problems they faced. They did not, however, find Zapata.

Zapata had left the city, presumably because he was ill, and given Palafox the authority to speak on his behalf. Palafox kept to the official *Zapatista* script, one he increasingly took charge of, and insisted that the Plan de Ayala had to be implemented without being changed. With both sides insisting that any concessions were unacceptable, negotiating an agreement became impossible. The only hope for the *Carrancistas* to establish authority over Morelos was that the state's war-wearied population would turn against Zapata for the sake of peace. Zapata's return to Cuernavaca did not change the position that Villarreal and Cabrera found themselves in, and their final meeting with Zapata, which took place as they were preparing to return to Mexico City, was hostile. Zapata angrily demanded that Carranza come to Morelos himself if he wanted real negotiations and insisted that the ideals for which the *Zapatistas* had fought would not be abandoned. Carranza would have to accept the Plan de Ayala and resign if he were to find allies among them.

The impasse in Cuernavaca did not put a stop to discussions, which continued until the beginning of September. After that, any hope of an agreement ended. Zapata went so far as to write to Blanco, "I tell you in all frankness that this Carranza does not inspire much confidence in me. I see in him much ambition and a disposition to fool people."[7] Soon after, on September 8, Zapata seemed to turn his attention to Morelos and began implementing the eighth provision of the Plan de Ayala, the one that stated that those opposed to the plan would lose their property, two thirds of which would be used to fund the war and provide pensions for the widows and orphans of dead *Zapatistas*. Thereafter, the process of redistributing land proceeded rapidly in the state. Zapata, in a letter to Woodrow Wilson, dated August 23, 1914, claimed that land repossession was taking place all over Mexico, including "in Morelos, Guerrero, Michoacán, Puebla, Tamaulipas, Nuevo León, Chihuahua, Sonora, Durango, Zacatecas, and San Luís Potosí,"[8] but Zapata was also quick to assure Wilson that foreigners' legitimate interests would be respected. If field reports about the issue, at least those originating in Morelos, can be believed, the redistribution was carried out with a sense of fairness—that is, with a concern for the historical division of property that the villages had always relied upon to defend their rights to certain fields. On September 19, for instance, Eufemio reported from Cuautla "that the irrigated land is already being suitably redistributed in the area surrounding this and other towns which have requested it. The people appointed to the task have an expert knowledge of the reference-system for redivision."[9]

As the *Zapatistas* were independently implementing their land-redistribution program, the conflict between Villa and Carranza heated up. Carranza approached Villa much as he had approached Zapata, that is, through a representative, sending General Obregón to Chihuahua in the middle of September to forge an accord. Carranza was obliged to appear receptive to Villa, who was an ally whose army had helped

Carranza achieve victory. Tensions between the two were not new, for Carranza saw Villa, who "broke the back of the federal army,"[10] as competition and had sought to rein him in during June, going so far as to slow an arms delivery to Villa's forces. The threat of a split between the two had obliged them, shortly before Huerta's resignation, to negotiate the Torreón Pact, a treaty that was meant to guarantee the unity of the two halves of the northern movement as certain victory approached. Obregón's goal at this moment was to require Villa to submit to Carranza's authority in return for the First Chief's living up to the agreement that had been signed in Torreón. In compliance with that agreement, Carranza proposed holding a revolutionary convention—details of which were contained in a letter that Obregón brought to Villa—on October 1. Both Villa and Obregón rejected the legitimacy of the proposed convention because the officers who were to participate would likely ignore the interests of the common soldiers and exclude such issues as agrarian reform. They told Carranza they disagreed in a letter dated September 21. The following day, Villa, unwilling to wait for Carranza to address his and Obregón's concerns, sent Carranza a telegram denying his legitimacy and then publicly declaring that Carranza had "[r]efused to accept a Convention on the bases proposed in the Torreón Pact."[11]

Carranza went ahead with his convention on October 1. Its delegates all supported him, and they confirmed his position as the revolutionary government's head. Villa now threatened to attack Mexico City, and Carranza, following Obregón's urging, agreed to hold another convention at Aguascalientes, a site that had been proposed by Blanco before the first convention as superior because it was "neutral ground."[12] The problem for Carranza was that he did not control this new convention, and within days, its delegates asserted their independence from the *Carrancistas*, declaring that they had sovereign authority, and invited Zapata to send a delegation. He ignored the invitation until two *Villista* generals, Felipe Ángeles and Calixto Contreras, went to Morelos to convince him of the value of working with the new convention. Zapata would not decide on his own, calling his chiefs to confer on the matter and collectively accept the invitation. The chiefs deferred, sending colonels to represent them, and Zapata was thus the only figure of importance at the meeting in which it was agreed to send delegates.

The *Zapatista* delegates arrived in Aguascalientes on October 27 but refused to participate in any discussions until the convention's members accepted the principles of the Plan de Ayala. The next day, most of the articles of Zapata's plan were adopted in a unanimous vote. Carranza then demanded that Villa and Zapata step down from their commands, something neither was about to do. On October 30, the convention voted to remove Carranza from his executive position. Villa was also relieved of his command, a provision he apparently allowed to come to a vote, and General Eutalio Gutiérrez was appointed interim president of a government that came to be known as the Convention. The convention dragged on for another week and a half, at which point Gutiérrez, whom the *Zapatistas* sarcastically called "*el presidente accidental*,"[13] declared Carranza a rebel and appointed Villa the head of the army. Despite his misgivings about the suitability of Carranza for the presidency, Obregón remained a *Carrancista* because he distrusted Villa, Gutiérrez, and the *Zapatistas*. The convention, therefore, ended with an open conflict between Gutiérrez's Conventionist government, which was supported by Villa's troops, and Carranza's Constitutionalist government, which was supported by Obregón's troops.

This split was not simply about two figures vying for power. Indeed, Gutiérrez, despite having proved a valuable revolutionary, had little experience with politics and his election was the result of a compromise—the reason that the *Zapatistas* called him the accidental president. His appointment did not alienate a significant portion of the delegates. The split between the Conventionists and Constitutionalists involved opposed visions of what the revolution was about, an opposition that had been creating difficulties among revolutionaries since 1911. Those who sided with the Conventionists wanted social change and saw the revolution as a means to effect that change, whereas the Constitutionalists—with the exception, at least to some extent, of Obregón—merely wanted to alter the country's political landscape, while leaving its social structure intact. The conflict between Zapata and Madero had been similar, and Villa now sought Zapata's help in securing victory for the Conventionists, informing Zapata 10 days before the convention had officially ended—on November 10—that "the time for hostilities has come."[14] Villa, who was planning to take Mexico City, wanted Zapata to mobilize his men and prevent the *Carrancistas* from reinforcing the troops they had in Mexico City with men from Veracruz, the city to which Carranza had retreated when he realized he had lost control of events in Aguascalientes.

Zapata agreed to Villa's request, moving from his headquarters in Cuernavaca and heading north to join his army on the outskirts of Mexico City, where Carranza's men continued in their standoff with the *Zapatistas*. That standoff persisted until November 24, when the last of the *Carrancistas* abandoned the city, and the *Zapatistas* moved in, establishing control for the Conventionists. Despite the terror within the capital over Zapata's arrival, the result of years of anti-*Zapatista* propaganda, the *Zapatistas* proved exceptionally well behaved, prompting those within the city to observe, "Zapata proved the *only* leader whose men did not loot, and were kept in order. . . . [I]t was possible to give almost any Zapata common soldier a bill to go on an errand, or make a purchase, and have the article and change duly returned."[15] Zapata arrived two days later by train, taking a room at the San Lázaro hotel, a modest establishment located near the train station. Disappointed that the victory that had toppled Huerta was turning out to be merely a transition into another conflict, Zapata avoided treating his present success as a victory, keeping away from the National Palace, where Eufemio stayed with his troops and where a celebratory reception had been planned. Zapata also avoided declaring victory to the press, responding to reporters who questioned him the day after he arrived with "an occasional 'yes' or 'no.'"[16]

Zapata's actions over the next few days further demonstrated his ambition was to found a government that accepted the principles of the Plan de Ayala. He himself had little interest in establishing a place for himself at the center of Mexican politics. Talks for arranging a meeting between Zapata and Villa, who remained outside the city in deference to Zapata,[17] were held between representatives of the two leaders, but the meeting would not occur in Mexico City, as Villa had hoped. Zapata, having secured the city, quickly returned home, arriving back in Cuernavaca on November 29. The *Zapatistas* stationed in the capital would follow their leader shortly thereafter, leaving it in the hands of the *Villistas*. Villa himself remained outside the city, though he did accompany Gutiérrez to the National Palace on December 3. With an eye toward establishing a stronger alliance with Zapata, Villa had intended to avoid occupying the capital on his own, and he now sent representatives to Cuernavaca to convince Zapata to return to it. Zapata refused to do so, arranging to confer with Villa in Xochimilco at a meeting that Leon Canova, a U.S. envoy who witnessed the event, described in detail for the U.S. State Department.

Villa arrived with a small escort, a sign of trust that Zapata seemed to appreciate, in Xochimilco around noon on December 4 to a festive atmosphere. A band played music, school children sang, and "So many were the bouquets and wreaths that our men could not carry them and our horses were walking on them while we rejoiced in our hearts," Villa wrote.[18] Montaño greeted him with a short speech in the town's center and then brought him to meet Zapata, who was waiting with Palafox, Eufemio, Amador Salazar, his sister María de Jesús, and his son Nicolás, who slept through the conference that followed in the nearby school building where Zapata and Villa sat down to talk. The business of negotiations began slowly, for the two men were bashful with each other. "It was interesting and amusing to watch Villa and Zapata trying to get acquainted with each other," Canova wrote. "For half an hour they sat in an embarrassed silence, occasionally broken by some insignificant remark, like two country sweethearts."[19] The ice didn't break until the subject of Carranza came up about a half hour into the conference. Villa denounced him as insolent, and Zapata rejoined, "I have always said that . . . that Carranza is a scoundrel."[20] They then became animated, discussing their opposition to Carranza and growing friendlier. "I am a man who doesn't like to fawn on anyone, but you surely know that I have been thinking about you for a long time," Villa offered. To which Zapata replied, "And we, too. Those who have gone up north, of the many who have gone . . . they have told me that things looked hopeful for me up there. He is, I said to myself, the only one I can count on."[21] The two talked on, touching on such subjects as agrarian reform, their unfitness for taking on the presidency, and their need to control whoever became president to ensure that proper reform was enacted. Zapata then had cognac brought in, and Villa, who was not a drinker, called for water, a request that dumbfounded Zapata and which he ignored, pouring two glasses and handing one to Villa, who drank it quickly and turned red and teary eyed as it hit his stomach.

Circa 1914: Mexican revolutionary Emiliano Zapata (foreground) assembles with his army of peasants and farmers on horseback, Mexico. (Hulton Archive/ Getty Images)

After such pleasantries were over, the two men, along with Palafox, retired to a private room to discuss their immediate problems, which included weeding out enemies from Huerta's government who had recently joined their ranks. They primarily focused on the coming battle against the *Carrancistas* and on how best to crush that movement quickly. Zapata, it was agreed, would capture and occupy Puebla City, which was strategically important if Villa were to be successful in taking Veracruz and finishing off Carranza. Villa also promised a generous supply of weapons, including heavy artillery, and ammunition not simply to solve the *Zapatistas* constant shortages but to give them significantly greater strength. The meeting concluded with Zapata agreeing to join Villa in Mexico City on December 6, when over 50,000 troops, a combination of *Zapatistas* and *Villistas*, paraded through the streets behind their two generals before appreciative crowds. Gutiérrez reviewed the troops at the *zócalo*, the city's large central square, but Zapata and Villa paid little attention to him, and when they entered the National Palace, Villa sat in the presidential chair, afterwards telling Zapata to take his place on it. "'I didn't fight for that. I fought to get the lands back. I don't care about politics.' And later he said, 'We should burn the

Chair to end ambitions.'"[22] Zapata left Mexico City three days after his arrival, likely confident that he and Villa would soon put an end to the threat of the *Carrancistas* and bring an end to the fighting.

That hope began to dwindle almost immediately. The artillery Villa had promised did not come as expected, forcing Zapata to repeatedly request it. When Villa did send it, Zapata's men had to haul it with the help of mules over the mountains, because Villa could not spare transport trains, to Puebla City, where it arrived on December 15. That same day, the *Zapatistas* moved into the city, taking control of it without opposition: the *Carrancistas* had fled as soon as they saw the fire power that they were up against. Meanwhile, in Mexico City, hostilities broke out between the *Villistas* and the *Zapatistas*, a sign of disunity that manifested itself even among high ranking *Villista* soldiers. Villa, for example, had Zapata's chief delegate to the Convention, Paulino Martínez, shot on December 13, and about 200 more people, civilians as well as *Zapatistas*, would be killed at the hands of *Villistas* by the end of the month. Zapata also began to hear that former federal agents, who hoped Carranza would emerge victorious, had infiltrated the revolutionary ranks and were spreading suspicion. "Our enemies are working very actively to divide the North and South," Zapata wrote to Villa, "for which reason I see myself compelled to recommend that you take the greatest care possible on this particular."[23] The formality of the message suggested a change in Zapata's confidence in his ally. Disgusted with the problems that were emerging in his alliance with Villa, Zapata soon withdrew from the national fight, abandoning, for the most part, Puebla City and returning to Morelos, where he withdrew to Tlaltizapán.

Zapata had not abandoned his fight for land reform. Rather, he turned his attention to local problems and focused on implementing his reform program within Morelos. He continued to ignore national politics as the situation grew increasingly bleak for those who had put their voices behind the Plan de Ayala in November. The conflict within the Convention widened. Villa was at odds with Gutiérrez, who thus reached out to the *Carrancistas* and began secret negotiations with Obregón, who took advantage of the disarray within the government and went on the offensive as 1914 turned to 1915. By the end of the first week of the new year, Obregón had retaken control of Puebla City, clearing it of the few *Zapatistas* who had remained there, and was well on his way to Mexico City. Consequently, Gutiérrez fled the city on January 16, and the *Villistas* named Roque González Garza, a Villista delegate in Aguascalientes, the acting executive, in lieu of appointing a new provisional president. The Convention fled to Morelos 10 days later, and the *Carrancistas* reestablished their control over the capital on January 28.

González Garza's government was now based in Cuernavaca. Consequently, the *Zapatistas* gained a more prominent influence on it, an influence González Garza would not be comfortable with for long. In the short term, Palafox became the agriculture minister and established and worked with commissions to study the land issue in every area of Morelos. About five weeks later, Zapata informed González Garza, "The matter relating to the agrarian question is resolved in a definitive manner, for the different pueblos of the state, in accord with the titles which protect their properties, have entered into the possession of said lands."[24] Zapata had tried his best to limit his focus to land redistribution, which did not always go smoothly, despite assertions to the contrary, because long-established conflicts between villages sometime manifested in arguments over what patch of land belonged to which village, but other issues inevitably got in the way. For example, the question about paying *Zapatista* soldiers, a practice that leading *Zapatistas* wanted to begin in order to further professionalize their army— was raised in early February. Zapata and González Garza did arrive at a solution: paymasters would distribute salaries. The issue, however, remained a problem for both men throughout February and March, as the amounts agreed upon were found to be inadequate by the *Zapatistas,* while González Garza saw their demands, in regard to payment of soldiers as well as other issues, as an intrusion upon his authority. Similarly, Zapata likely felt González Garza's attempts to impose his authority on Morelos unacceptable.

Less than two months after fleeing, the Convention returned on March 21, 1915, to Mexico City. Obregón had abandoned the capital 10 days earlier, having decided that holding it was not worthwhile, especially because the Convention had successfully maintained a blockade that caused extreme want. "It was a time of filth and pestilence. The city was full of lice, and there was a terrific epidemic of typhus fever. We all had to join together in the support of soup kitchens in Mexico City and the suburbs; the poor people were absolutely starving. In her entire history Mexico has perhaps never experienced such widespread privation as during that long winter of 1915."[25] The return of the Convention thus brought Mexico City a sense of hope, something González Garza must also have felt—he must have believed that he would be free of the *Zapatistas'* influence once he got out of Morelos. He would soon be disappointed, for Palafox, whose ambition was to maneuver his way into higher office, continued attempting to impose his will on the Convention.

Zapata, by contrast, was freed from the Convention's meddling, and he now became even more focused on local problems, an element of his disposition at that time that led Duval West, an American judge who had been sent to Mexico on a fact-finding mission by President Wilson, to see Zapata's approach to the Revolution as naive. West arrived in Morelos on April 16. Although Zapata did discuss with him issues involving Mexico as a whole, West left with the impression that Zapata's "influence will eventually be narrowed to the people in the country he represents."[26] He went on to observe that Zapata imagined victory in these terms: "All men, he said, should carry their arms as they till the fields. If the enemy should come, then the men must leave their occupations to defeat him. Life to Zapata was the soil, the air, the mountains of Morelos. And for these ideals—land and liberty—he led his revolutionary movement."[27] González Garza's need for Zapata to be interested in what was happening outside Morelos during that time became more urgent, and he sent telegrams almost every day in April to Zapata, only to have them ignored or answered in a disinterested fashion.

NOTES

1. For a discussion of the similarities and differences between Zapata and Villa, see Friedrich Katz, "The Agrarian Policies and Ideas of the Revolutionary Mexican Factions Led by Emiliano Zapata, Pancho Villa and Venustiano Carranza," in *Reforming Mexico's Agrarian Reform,* ed. Laura Randall (Armonk, NY: M. E. Sharpe, 1996), 21–35. Perhaps the most relevant passage, for our purposes, notes, "There

were significant similarities between the agrarian policies of . . . Zapata and Villa. In both cases the large haciendas . . . were confiscated. In both cases the leaders . . . stated that the hacendados would never be allowed to return, and in both cases they promised to divide the lands among their respective peasantries. The great difference . . . was that in Morelos . . . land was effectively distributed to village communities, while only a limited land distribution was carried out in the Villista-held territories, and the largest estates remained under state administration" (28).

2. For Carranza's consideration of Zapata as rabble prior to his ascent to power, see Frank McLynn, *Villa and Zapata: A History of the Mexican Revolution* (New York: Carroll & Graf, 2002), 246–47 and Robert P. Millon, *The Ideology of a Peasant Revolution* (New York: International, 1995 [1969]) in which Carranza's private secretary describes Carranza's view of joining the Constitutionalists to the *Zapatistas* "as the abominable union with the rabble of Zapata" (Millon, *Ideology of a Peasant Revolution*, 24). Later, Carranza continued to refer to the Liberating Army of the South as "the Zapata rabble." See Bill Weinberg, *Homage to Chiapas: The New Indigenous Struggles in Mexico* (London: Verso, 2000), 55.

3. Quoted in Adolfo Gilly, *The Mexican Revolution*, trans. Patrick Camiller (New York: New Press, 2005 [1971]), 129.

4. Quoted in Millon, *Ideology of a Peasant Revolution*, 25. The Plan of Guadalupe was Carranza's revolutionary doctrine. Issued in March 1913, it proposed solving Mexico's inequalities through the power of the country's constitution, and thus Carranza came to seem very much like Madero, and the campesinos came to see him, according to the Mexican historian Arnaldo Cordova, as "twice a traitor:—traitor, because he has sold the fatherland; traitor, because he has sold it to the hacendados." Quoted in Steven E. Sanderson, *Agrarian Populism and the Mexican State: The Struggle for Land in Sonora* (Berkeley: University of California Press, 1981), 72.

5. Some *Carrancistas*, for instance, Carranza's chief of staff Juan Barragán Rodrígues, claimed that the *Zapatistas'* insistence that the Plan de Ayala be accepted without change prevented the two groups from uniting, as article II of that plan named Zapata as the leader of the revolution. The argument was made during the revolution "but it

was only until sometime after the armed conflict ended that it became fashionable" (Millon, *Ideology of a Peasant Revolution*, 136).

6. Quoted in Samuel Brunk, *Emiliano Zapata! Revolution and Betrayal in Mexico* (Albuquerque: University of New Mexico Press, 1995), 119.

7. Quoted in McLynn, *Villa and Zapata*, 251.

8. Millon, *Ideology of a Peasant Revolution*, 52. For Zapata's addressing the United States' concerns about the interests of foreign investors, an issue that had determined and would continue to determine U.S. policy toward Mexico, see Brunk's *Emiliano Zapata*, 174, 308n7.

9. Quoted in Gilly, *Mexican Revolution*, 128.

10. Millon, *Ideology of a Peasant Revolution*, 20.

11. Quoted in Gilly, *Mexican Revolution*, 138.

12. Ibid.

13. Quoted in Ronald Atkin, *Revolution: Mexico 1910–20* (New York: John Fay, 1970), 226.

14. Quoted in John Womack, *Zapata and the Mexican Revolution* (New York: Vintage Books, 1970 [1968]), 219.

15. William E. Gates, "The Four Governments of Mexico: Zapata—Protector of Morelos," in *The World's Work*, vol. 37 (New York: Doubleday, Page, 1919), 665.

16. Robert E. Quirk, *The Mexican Revolution, 1914–1915* (New York: W. W. Norton, 1970 [1960]), 133.

17. As Atkin puts it, "Villa was determined not to repeat the mistake made by Carranza in occupying Mexico City in the face of Zapata" (*Revolution*, 232).

18. Atkin, *Revolution*, 232.

19. Quoted in McLynn, *Villa and Zapata*, 275.

20. Quoted in Quirk, *Mexican Revolution*, 136.

21. Ibid., 138.

22. Quoted in Enrique Krauze, *Mexico: Biography of Power; A History of Modern Mexico, 1810–1996*, trans. Hank Heifetz (New York: HarperCollins, 1998), 295.

23. Quoted in Roger Parkinson, *Zapata: A Biography* (Briarcliff Manor, NY: Stein & Day, 1980 [1975]), 201.

24. Quoted in Womack, *Zapata and the Mexican Revolution*, 234–35.

25. Leone B. Moats, *Thunder in Their Veins: A Memoir of Mexico* (New York: Century, 1932), 170–71.

26. Quoted in Quirk, *Mexican Revolution*, 230.

27. Ibid.

Chapter 8

STARTING OVER AGAIN

The Convention's army was now, in practice if not in theory, almost exclusively *Villista*. It had acquired a reputation for invincibility during the first months of 1915, but, as Zapata isolated himself from the nation, it was forced into retreat. The turning point for the *Villistas* came at the battle of Celaya on April 6 and 7. Engaging Obregón against the advice of Ángeles, Villa appeared poised for victory after Obregón's frontline, early in the battle, attempted to take a position that was unknowingly occupied by *Villistas*, who forced the advancing troops to fall back in disarray. Obregón, seeing disorder among his men, guessed that Villa would react by attacking. To build Villa's confidence, Obregón made it seem as if there were greater confusion than there actually was. Villa fell for the trick. Hoping to end the battle quickly, he ordered his cavalry to attack without first providing it with cover, and the unprotected *Villistas* were cut down by machine-gun fire. Villa, rather than reconsider his approach, ordered more cavalry forward, something he continued to do until dusk, starting up again the following day. On the afternoon of the seventh, the *Villistas* ran out of ammunition, and Obregón counterattacked using cavalry he had kept in reserve. The exhausted *Villistas*, lacking a reserve, were routed and suffered heavy losses. Villa refused to accept defeat. Three days after his retreat, a *Villista* paper asserted, "Obregón has failed in his attempt to break the Villista line of fire."[1]

Intent on demonstrating the truth of his press's propaganda, Villa returned to Celaya on April 13 with 25,000 troops, 10,000 more than Obregón had with him. But Villa followed the same plan of attack that had proved so ineffective the previous week, and Obregón, who had predicted Villa would return, had strengthened his defenses, reinforcing his troops and his machine guns. Line after line of *Villistas* rushed the *Obregonistas'* positions for two days, getting slaughtered as they did so, and at dawn on April 15, Obregón ordered cavalry that had been kept in reserve to attack, forcing Villa and his army to flee north. The size of the *Villistas* was reduced by as many as 10,000 men, about 3,000 of whom died, while the others were either wounded or captured. But Villa had not yet exhausted his resources. Over the next two weeks, he was able to replenish his army, making it about as large as it had been in March, to prepare for the next battle. Villa's army met Obregón's for a third time at the end of April in the 12-mile stretch between Trinidad and León de los Aldamas. Although he took the role of the aggressor, Villa showed restraint, positioning his men in trenches just as Obregón had been doing. For a little more than three weeks, the two sides engaged each other in little more than skirmishes. Neither side was able to take the upper hand. But Villa grew impatient, and on May 22, he attacked Obregón's lines head on, failing to break through the enemy's defenses. Ten more days passed with little action. Villa again attacked and again failed to defeat the *Obregonistas,* who counterattacked on June 5 and forced the *Villistas* to retreat farther north. The *Villistas'* threat to Carranza, while not eliminated, had been contained.

Zapata's inactivity had been a great help to Obregón, particularly during his buildup to the Celaya battle. Villa failed to recognize the extent of Zapata's withdrawal from the Convention, a withdrawal that was partially the result of his inability to mobilize his forces for battles outside Morelos. Villa had expected Zapata to cut Veracruz off from the north, preventing Obregón from communicating with Carranza and resupplying his troops.[2] Zapata's forces did practically nothing, showing almost complete indifference to protecting the gains of the revolution. They did launch minor attacks on Obregón's forces while the battle of

Trinidad was taking place, destroying, on May 12, the railroad track that Carranza had been using to send supplies north and sometimes defeating northward bound units. But such actions proved minor annoyances, doing little to disrupt the Constitutionalists' progress. It wasn't until Zapata began to fear that Obregón might wipe out the *Villistas* and allow Carranza to turn his full attention to Morelos that the *Zapatistas* began to attack the Constitutionalists flanks,[3] but by that point, the battle for Trinidad was practically over. The Constitutionalists had done almost everything they would need to do to take control of the country, even though the Conventionists remained in Mexico City, technically serving as the official government.

Zapata needed the Convention government to remain in power in order to achieve what he wanted. The *Zapatistas'* return to action against the *Carrancistas* in May followed an episode that demonstrated Zapata's interest in what was going on in Mexico City, despite his and his follower's lack of engagement. *Zapatistas*, in fact, had remained in the government and had actually held a majority of the seats in the Convention's cabinet. The most prominent among those holding office was Palafox, who continued serving as the agricultural minister. The influence that he would be able to exert offered Zapata the only real hope that his land-reform measures could become federal law, but Palafox had little patience with the slow pace of reform and confronted González Garza a number of times over the Convention's lack of action. Those confrontations alienated the other members of the government, hindering Palafox's ability to get things done. The most dramatic confrontation took place on April 7, when Palafox stormed into the office of González Garza and accused him of holding back the work of reform. González Garza responded by demanding Palafox's resignation but was dissuaded from enforcing his demand by Soto y Gama and Adalberto Hernández, the undersecretary of agriculture. By April 30, however, González Garza had had enough of Palafox and held a secret meeting at which he sought and received the Convention's permission to remove Palafox.

Although Zapata had been informed by González Garza of his issues with Palafox, he was not prepared to allow his most important intellectual to be removed from office. When he learned of the vote on May 2, Zapata wrote to González Garza, ordering him not to act on it and arranging to go to Mexico City to ensure that Palafox continued serving as the agricultural minister. Zapata arrived two days later, and González Garza, accompanied by a single aide, met him at Los Reyes. He refused to back down, insisting that as the government's provisional leader he was in charge—even after Zapata drew his pistol. The two traveled together to Mexico City, and Zapata continued to argue his case. González Garza publicly insisted on his status as the country's legitimate leader, but some compromise must have been settled upon. Within hours, Zapata was traveling back to Morelos by train, having ridden his horse onto a railroad wagon and departed Mexico City for the last time. Palafox would keep his position. Nevertheless, the relationship between González Garza and those *Zapatistas* who sided with Palafox remained tense. On May 7, for instance, the *Zapatista* Antonio Barona shot and killed Francisco Estrada, González Garza's chief of staff, and then went to the Hotel Lascuraín, purportedly to find Juan Banderas, a *Villista* general who had been involved in attacks on the *Zapatistas* in December of the previous year. González Garza was also living at the hotel, and it was widely reported that he had also been a target, despite Zapata's and Villa's assertions to the contrary.[4]

Zapata now remained holed up in his headquarters in Tlaltizapán, and with the exception of ordering his men to engage the *Carrancistas* that were heading north, he focused on Morelos. The situation had changed enough after Villa's defeat that, on June 18, Zapata saw the urgency of helping defend the Convention, and he called for "all generals, chiefs, and officers of the Liberating Army, who are passing their time in Mexico City in theaters, cantinas, and houses of ill fame, to report at the front for duty."[5] By this time, González Garza was no longer the acting executive, having been replaced nine days earlier by Francisco Lagos Cházaro. Furthermore, Pablo González, the Carranza's general who was operating in the south and held the distinction of having never won a battle, was moving toward Mexico City. His progress was somewhat delayed by the *Zapatistas'* stand under the command of Rafael Eguía Lis at Gran Canal, 15 miles from the capital. On June 24, despite being poorly armed, these men managed to push back González, although their lack of ammunition forced them to withdraw not long after, and González continued advancing, entering the city on July 11, four days after the Convention convened in the capital for the last time. It would soon reconvene in Toluca. The Convention had been thrown out of Mexico's capital by the most ineffective general in the country.

González did not take his victory for granted. Over the next three weeks, uncertainty remained over who would ultimately succeed in holding Mexico City. González pulled his troops out of the city on the 17th, fearing a Conventionist counterattack, and the *Zapatistas* soon moved in, but their occupation was chaotic. No rule of law was established, and any rumor that the Constitutionalists were preparing to attack caused them to flee south. Zapata now returned to action, riding toward the capital at the end of July with about 6,000 men in order to rid the region of *Carrancistas*. But Zapata's men were not well armed and failed to coordinate their efforts with *Villistas*, who remained active despite their losses earlier in the year. They had sought out Zapata to help prevent Obregón from moving farther north and capturing Villa, who was now pinning his hopes on brokering a peace deal among all revolutionary groups in an attempt to win U.S. support. Zapata, unable to coordinate attacks with *Villistas*, saw that military engagement was futile and retreated. González returned to Mexico City on August 2. Soon after, Carranza moved into the National Palace, and he would still be there when Zapata's revolutionary career was brought to an end four years later. For the moment, Zapata waited, hoping that a conference on the Mexican problem in Washington, D.C., would lead to the unification of the various revolutionary factions and the removal of Carranza from office, a notion that Soto y Gama had encouraged Zapata to believe. The other possibility that Zapata considered was that Obregón would turn on Carranza, throwing him out of office, and join the Convention.

Zapata's optimism regarding the Washington conference seems quixotic. First, Carranza refused to participate, leading the U.S. secretary of state, Robert Lansing, to ask President Wilson, "Are we bound to call a conference when only the defeated factions have accepted?"[6] Second, the U.S. government misunderstood the problem, something that President Wilson made obvious in a statement he released on the Mexican issue at the beginning of June, copies of which were sent to Zapata, as well as to Carranza, Villa, and González Garza. Wilson—apparently regarding the factionalism among the revolutionaries as the result of each party's desire to seize control of the country—observed, "All profess the same objects, they are, nevertheless, unable or unwilling to cooperate. A central authority at Mexico City is no sooner set up than it is undermined and its authority defied by those who were expected to support it. Mexico is no nearer a solution of her tragical troubles than she was when the revolution was first kindled."[7] The lack of a solution, in fact, was a result of the different goals of the various leaders, and the *Zapatistas'* opposition to the authority that Zapata was "expected to support" had nothing to do with any aspirations that he harbored beyond ensuring that land reform was carried out. His belief that Obregón might still join the Convention was more realistic. Obregón, after all, had helped convince Carranza the previous October to participate in the Aguascalientes convention, had accepted the Plan de Ayala's principles when the issue was voted on at that convention, and had more recently worked toward improving the lives of the poorer classes—establishing labor unions, for example, in the cities he gained control over during his hunt for Villa. Zapata simply could not know the depth of Obregón's mistrust of him.

Zapata did not rely on hope for too long. Unable to wait for outside forces to resolve the problems he faced, he resumed his offensive in September, but his forces were held back by their usual shortage of weapons and ammunition, and they were unable to do much more than launch raids on the Federal District and Mexico State. Towns were briefly occupied and the Necaxa power plant, an energy source for Mexico City, was captured at the end of the month, but these victories were short-term triumphs that did little to improve Zapata's position. The odds against him increased in October, partially as a result of Villa's failures. Villa had been struggling to regain the initiative in the north, but he suffered defeat in town after town and was driven farther from Mexico City. The U.S. government now felt obliged to treat Carranza as the legitimate ruler—even though full recognition of his government would not be granted until March 1917—and it prohibited arms being shipped to other revolutionary factions. Admitting defeat, the Conventionist government disbanded, putting an end to a movement that linked *Zapatismo* to the rest of Mexico. Zapata, however, was not ready to give up his pretensions to being part of a nationwide power.

On October 19, the *Zapatista* faction of the Convention, in a ceremony presided over by Zapata, set up a shadow government in Cuernavaca—one with no real power outside Morelos—under the leadership of Palafox. This government continued, at Zapata's request, to act as if it had real power, enacting legislation for the entire country.

The first of the new Conventionist government's decrees was made the following week. Palafox published on October 26 *A Manifesto to the Nation*, a new reform program that he likely wrote with Soto y Gama. The manifesto detailed the improvements that the Conventionists planned for the nation, making pronouncements on issues ranging from taxes, land, education, and labor to divorce. Many of the promised reforms had been approved by the entire Convention in Toluca, but they now became part of the *Zapatista* revolutionary program, proving that *Zapatismo* would offer solutions to problems that the Plan de Ayala had not addressed. Palafox and Soto y Gama enacted an agrarian law as well. It set a maximum size for farms—although in consideration of the differences in land quality from place to place, the approved size varied, ranging from 247 acres of the best land to 2,471 acres of the poorest. The law also made rules about villages' use of water, giving precedence to the needs of farmers, as well as rules about land use: families holding farms were required to farm them themselves—an obvious attack on the peonage system—and land that was left fallow for more than two years would be appropriated by the villages to which it belonged and be available for redistribution.

These publications, which were meant to serve as propaganda outside Morelos and to demonstrate to the peasant and working classes the radical difference between *Zapatismo* and *Carrancismo*, actually revealed a gap between *Zapatista* thinking and that of the rest of the nation. The manifesto and the law attempted to focus the people's rage against the hacendados, who, as the historian John Womack notes, "no longer had power in Mexico. Most languished in jail or exile. As a class they hardly even existed. True, outside Morelos the nation's villages had not emerged dominant. But the state and district chiefs who led them were not likely to champion agrarian revolt now, since thanks to Carranza precisely they had become the new landlords."[8] Furthermore, Obregón had instituted his own populist policies, decreeing "a minimum wage for all areas under Carranza's control" and thereby gaining the support

of many who would have been more likely to join the *Villistas* or *Zapatistas*.[9] *Zapatismo* had not accommodated itself to the changes that the
revolution had brought to Mexico, retaining rhetorical strategies that
had been useful when Díaz or Huerta was in control but that were no
longer effective. The movement's objective remained relevant but new
ways to talk about it needed to be found if those who would benefit
from reaching it, at least outside Morelos, were to listen.[10]

Zapata faced a different problem within Morelos. The success of
his land program over the previous year, coupled with the quality of
the harvest in 1915, had produced widespread contentment among the
campesinos and made gathering support for another fight among the
state's population difficult.[11] Carranza was thus able to put Morelos in
the back of his mind while he consolidated his control over the rest
of the country. He didn't completely ignore Morelos, sending 10,000
troops in an attempt to breach the state's well-defended borders and
establish a presence in it that would be useful when he could more

*The Agrarian Revolution of Emiliano Zapata, from Porfirianism to the Revolu-
tion (Dal porfirismo a la revolucion), by David Alfaro Siqueiros (1896–1974),
1964. (Schalkwijk/Art Resource)*

fully invest his resources in it. The situation produced a conundrum for Zapata. So long as his generals could defend the border and keep the *Carrancistas* out of Morelos, the relative peace within the state would be maintained and the ordinary campesinos would see no need to risk their lives or livelihoods in support of the *Zapatistas*, but if the *Carrancistas* did successfully breach the border defenses, the *Zapatistas* would find themselves on the defensive, little better off than they had been two years before. They would also lack the ability to continue fighting the *Carrancistas* on the scale that they had been doing and would be unable to prepare for the larger force that they expected would come. Maintaining *Zapatista* dominance in Morelos thus proved both a hindrance and a help to the revolutionary effort.

Certainly the most positive element of keeping Morelos from coming under *Carrancista* control was that it allowed the *Zapatistas* to remain the de facto governors of the state, permitting them to function like a government and develop what the historian Frank McLynn describes as something of a "peasant utopia,"[12] despite abuses against villagers committed by *Zapatistas* who needed supplies. The *Zapatistas* printed money that served as legal tender in the state until early spring 1916, although, as the *Carrancistas'* imminent arrival came closer, the currency became less useful: people feared that using the money would be regarded as a sign of collaboration. Zapata also established a munitions factory, which was first located at the Atlihuayán hacienda but was later moved to Tlaltizapán. No longer able to acquire either ammunition or weapons from U.S. sources, the *Zapatistas* filled cartridges with copper at the factory, using wire taken from tram lines in Mexico City, and thereby managed to relieve their forces of the shortages they suffered. The ammunition that was produced was far from perfect, proving ineffective at long range, but it was better than nothing. Indeed, it was good enough to help Zapata's generals keep out the *Carrancistas*, whom Carranza promised at the end of November would chase down the *Zapatistas* "right into their hideouts in . . . Morelos."[13] De la O proved exceptional in defending against incursions, driving *Carrancista* forces out of towns they had taken along the Puebla border and pushing them as far back as Acapulco. The other generals also held their own along the borders, and a successful resistance was maintained some months into 1916.

Another issue Zapata had to contend with was preserving the unity of the *Zapatista* resistance, a task that involved maintaining the peace among his generals and ensuring their continued loyalty to him. In August, Carranza made an amnesty offer to revolutionaries who would agree to put down their arms, and although Zapata warned his generals that the offer's goal was "to deepen the personal enmities which exist between chiefs . . . which we must avoid at all costs,"[14] some gave in to the temptation to get out of the fight, possibly because their followers did not want to continue. Discontent among leading *Zapatistas* had been evident much earlier in the year, something that was made particularly clear in May when the Convention, despite its containing a *Zapatista* majority, voted to remove Palafox from office. But more dangerous conflicts were simmering closer to home. De la O, for example, had lost the governorship and seemed to turn his back on the revolution in the spring, demobilizing his men and allowing them to tend to their land even though they were needed on the battlefield. Zapata, therefore, was forced to indulge him in order to keep him from joining the ranks of the *pacíficos*. At times, the problem of infighting among chiefs was entwined with the issue of loyalty: chiefs would attack rivals by questioning their commitment to Zapata, who would risk alienating a trustworthy ally by investigating false reports. For example, Francisco Mendoza, one of the chiefs who had signed the Plan de Ayala, became so frustrated by rivals' questioning him and the problems it caused him with the central leadership that he had told Zapata to assign a new chief to the state's southeastern zone, the region that he oversaw.

Perhaps the biggest question hanging over Zapata's head at the end of 1915 regarded the faithfulness of Francisco Pacheco. Pacheco served as the secretary of war for the Convention and for the *Zapatistas* after the Convention fell apart and was in charge of securing Morelos's northern border with Mexico State. Pacheco had shown increasing frustration with Zapata throughout 1915, complaining in August, "My face burns with the memory of how many times the enemy has driven us from the City [of Mexico], everyone running for Cuernavaca, committing intolerable abuses due to lack of discipline." He went on to question Zapata's leadership in more striking terms, asking "Who if not you, *compañero*, is in a position to prevent this and to admonish the Jefes who allow it?"[15] In November, Zapata had to coax Pacheco into staying on as the minister of war, but his obvious discontent did not abate. He complained about the lack of respect given to him. He felt Zapata had favored de la O in a feud that had been simmering between the two since 1912 over a land dispute involving de La O's village, Santa María, and Pacheco's village, Huitzilac. Pacheco also resented that his men, as all *Zapatista* soldiers throughout the ranks, were being forced to go without regular wages. In fact, regular wages, considered a benefit to being a *Zapatista*, would soon be discontinued. Pacheco's complaints were perhaps not as troubling as the fact that many of those who were defecting to the *Carrancistas* were men that Pacheco had recruited. His loyalty increasingly came under scrutiny well into 1916, but Zapata continued to put his trust in Pacheco, attempting to demonstrate to him his value to the *Zapatistas*. The strategic importance of his area of operations, after all, would turn losing him into a disaster.

NOTES

1. Quoted in Friedrich Katz, *The Life and Times of Pancho Villa* (Stanford, CA: Stanford University Press, 1998), 429.

2. See Katz, *Life and Times of Pancho Villa*, 497.

3. See Frank McLynn, *Villa and Zapata: A History of the Mexican Revolution* (New York: Carroll & Graf, 2002), 302.

4. The press asserted that Barona intended to assassinate González Garza. According to the New York *Independent*'s summary of the news from Mexico, "Barona, with a considerable following, attempted to assassinate President Garza, but the attacking force was driven back by Garza's guard" (82, no. 34670 [May 17, 1915], 275).

5. Quoted in Robert E. Quirk, *The Mexican Revolution, 1914–1915* (New York: W. W. Norton, 1970 [1960]), 269.

6. Ibid., 287.

7. *Information Annual*, 1915 (New York: R. R. Bowker, 1916), 382.

8. John Womack, *Zapata and the Mexican Revolution* (New York: Vintage Books, 1970 [1968]), 247.

9. Donald C. Hodges and Ross Gandy, *Mexico, the End of the Revolution* (Westport, CT: Praeger, 2002), 30.

10. Zapata, of course, had little time to worry about rhetoric, though he was concerned that his intellectuals did not distort the basic elements of *Zapatismo*. Thus *Zapatista* pronouncements would not have attempted to displace Zapata's message, but one should avoid equating the thinking of Zapata with that of his intellectuals, for example Palafox or Soto y Gama, who were both socialist. It is important to recognize that Zapata was, in some sense, a capitalist, though one who opposed large scale capitalist methods of farming, that is., that which was practiced by the haciendas, and favored small scale entrepreneurial operations instead. On this point see McLynn, *Villa and Zapata*, 270, and Samuel Brunk, *Emiliano Zapata! Revolution and Betrayal* (Albuquerque: University of New Mexico Press, 1995), 68.

11. Friedrich Katz, discussing how Villa, unlike Zapata, avoided land redistribution until the revolution was successful, aptly describes Zapata's problem in 1914: "An immediate land reform could easily have led to his [Villa's] soldiers returning home to secure their lands and refusing to fight outside their communities." See "The Agrarian Policies and Ideas of the Revolutionary Mexican Factions Led by Emiliano Zapata, Pancho Villa and Venustiano Carranza," in *Reforming Mexico's Agrarian Reform*, ed. Laura Randall (Armonk, NY: M. E. Sharpe, 1996), 29.

12. McLynn, *Villa and Zapata*, 270.

13. Womack, *Zapata and the Mexican Revolution*, 248.

14. Ibid.

15. Quoted in Brunk, *Emiliano Zapata!*, 187.

Chapter 9

THE BATTLE FOR MORELOS

During the last few months of 1915, Carranza had established control over Mexico. Pockets of resistance still existed—for example, the brothers Cedillo (Cleofas, Magdaleno, and Saturnino), who were allies of Villa, continued to fight in San Luis Potosí—but none seemed as dangerous as the one in Morelos, if only because of the wealth its sugar plantations were capable of producing.[1] Carranza could thus turn the full attention of his army to that state as the year came to a close and the new year began. He expected the Morelos problem to be solved quickly, observing in a speech on January 2, 1916, "The military struggle is now almost ended. The most important forces of the Reaction have been defeated and dispersed in the north, and there remains only that which is not Reaction, which is not anything: *Zapatismo*, composed of hordes of bandits, of men without consciences who cannot defeat our forces."[2] Carranza was so confident that he did not immediately expand the 10,000 strong force that was already amassed along Morelos's borders. Such confidence was belied by the fact that Zapata's generals continued to keep them at bay throughout January, and on February 1, 1916, the government announced that 20,000 more troops would soon be sent to reinforce those that were already surrounding the region. The time Zapata had for fully mobilizing the population of Morelos was quickly coming to an end. On February 7, he published another manifesto, asserting that the fight needed to continue because of the "boundless ambition of one man of unhealthy passions and no conscience,"[3] that is, Carranza.

Even with the reinforcements, Morelos's borders were not immediately opened, and events in the north soon suggested that Carranza would be safer if the Morelos campaign could be ended quickly. In March, Villa remained at large despite his defeat, and he tried to revive his fortunes with a raid in Columbus, New Mexico. He and his men killed 17 U.S. citizens, provoking the United States to seek permission to pursue Villa inside Mexico's borders. After Carranza agreed, with some conditions that were never met by the United States, President Wilson sent General John J. Pershing across the border with 10,000 men. This gave Villa, who could not be caught, a propaganda tool. Villa had been asserting that Carranza was working in league with the U.S. government and that his rule would eventually cause Mexican sovereignty to be undermined. The presence of U.S. troops on Mexican soil without resistance from Carranza's government could be seen as confirmation of that assertion. Villa's reputation among ordinary Mexicans in the north was boosted, and after some months, Carranza was forced to respond to the U.S. incursion, sending troops to oppose the Americans and face two enemies, the United States and the *Villistas*, simultaneously. Thereafter, historian Friedrich Katz observes, "Relations between the United States and Carranza deteriorated to such a degree that the Wilson administration imposed an arms embargo on the Carranza administration and American banks did not grant him any loans. Carranza thus became too weak to carry out his agenda of destroying the still rebellious peasant movements in Mexico and returning all the confiscated estates to their former owners."[4] The tension between Carranza's government and the United States would be smoothed over by the end of the year, although negotiations had twice failed earlier because Carranza could not agree to the U.S. demand to have "the right to return in the case of further border incidents," as the Mexican historian Adolfo Gilly notes.[5] The U.S. army, in any case, would return home at beginning of 1917, but its presence had already caused damage. Many of Mexico's peasant movements, including Villa's, the

Cedillo brothers', and Zapata's, even after Zapata died in 1919, would survive longer than Carranza.

Back in February 1916, the *Zapatistas* knew only that they would soon be facing a 30,000 strong force. Those close to Zapata remained optimistic, or at least they avoided displays of pessimism. Palafox, for example, discussed a time when they would "dominate Mexico City and other regions of the country," noting that when the time came "a great number of agrarian commissions will form, so that they will go into all the states of the Republic."[6] Doubts among the men in the field remained. In fact, defections had increased after Carranza's boast in November 1915 that the coming campaign against the *Zapatistas* would be definitive, reaching into their hideouts. Zapata turned to Pacheco as the crisis became more serious, sending him, as early as December, on a mission to negotiate with Pablo González, whose headquarters were located in the Federal District. The exact nature of these negotiations is not known, although the historian Samuel Brunk conjectures that Zapata was attempting to convince González to join the *Zapatistas* or to put Pacheco in a position to kill him. Whatever Zapata's intention, Pacheco was still in contact with González in late February, when de la O discovered what was happening. Fearing Pacheco was acting on his own, de la O began to take measures to prevent Pacheco's betraying the cause, warning him of the price of treason.[7] Zapata intervened; insisting on Pacheco's loyalty, he informed de la O that Pacheco was acting on instructions. Zapata, however, had his own doubts and asked de la O to keep an eye on the situation. Pacheco's discontent with his position was more apparent: he again began complaining, this time more vocally, about his soldiers' lack of pay, an issue that had nothing to do with Zapata's understanding of Pacheco's importance. It was a problem that everyone was facing and that would only get worse in the near future, as Zapata must have already known: all *Zapatistas* would lose their salaries in April.

Zapata needed to keep Pacheco from defecting and, to do so, promised to address personally the land dispute between Santa María and Huitzilac, that is, between de la O's and Pacheco's villages. The possibility that Pacheco would not remain loyal became clear on March 13, when he retreated from Huitzila, allowing the *Carrancistas* to attack. Zapata was still not ready to give up on Pacheco, but he also could not ignore the situation. He headed north to take charge of the attempt to cut off the advancing *Carrancistas*. At the same time, he continued to offer Pacheco reassurances, and he insisted that de la O, who was calling for Pacheco to be condemned as a traitor, find definitive proof of the treachery. Pacheco had not cut off communications with Zapata, writing to him about a plan to move his soldiers behind the advancing army, a move that would have enabled the *Zapatistas* to surround González's troops, if Pacheco were trustworthy, but one that would have allowed Pacheco to escape Zapata's reach, if he were a traitor. Before the plan could be put into action—a plan Zapata rejected—one of de la O's generals, Rafael Castillo, assassinated Pacheco in Miacatlán, an assassination Zapata sanctioned, evidently retroactively, rewarding de la O with provisions and money for his troops.

Justice may have been served, but the damage had been done, damage it would have been difficult to avoid so long as Pacheco chose to defect. Zapata had relied on Pacheco because of the value of the man's territory. Pacheco had been responsible for defending the mountainous region that served as a natural barrier between Mexico State and Morelos, and when he withdrew, the *Carrancistas* were given easy access to Morelos along a difficult-to-attack passage. Zapata could do nothing to stop the flow of *Carrancistas*, and they reached the suburbs of Cuernavaca by early April. The *Zapatistas* remained in control of that city for the rest of the month, because it took González until April 29 to marshal his resources, that is, to get heavy artillery into position in the hills surrounding the city—which offered good defenses against infantry but not against a bombardment from heavy guns—and begin the final push. By that time, Zapata had arrived to take charge of the state capital's defense, but his astuteness as a general was no match for the *Carrancistas'* greater military power. On May 2, González captured the city, Zapata having escaped the previous day and returned to his headquarters in Tlaltizapán. During the previous month, on April 16, the *Zapatistas* had suffered yet another blow, the likes of which the *Zapatistas* had not faced since Robles' attempted to wipe them out during Huerta's presidency. Amador Salazar, Zapata's cousin and an important *Zapatista* general, was killed by a stray bullet while on horseback during a confrontation at Yautepec. He remained upright, no one noticing he had died until his sombrero slipped off. Things only got worse:

after Cuernavaca fell, so too did most of the state's other major towns. Only Jojutla, Tlaltizapán, and a few villages remained under *Zapatista* control.

González proceeded to make the mistake that Robles and others had made, treating the entire population of Morelos as the enemy. He had women deported to work camps and men conscripted into the army, as well as executing both adults and children: in Tlaltizapán, which fell to his forces in mid-June, 132 men, 112 women, and 42 children were put to death. The executions were typical in their arbitrariness: those who were executed were guilty only of living in the village where Zapata kept his headquarters, the location of which was known to all. Those uninterested in fighting were therefore forced to flee, and a new unity emerged among the rural population. As the village of Tehuztla was evacuated, for example, one commentator remarked,

> People's faces were furious. They would barely mumble out a few words, but everyone had violent remarks for the Constitutional-ists on the tip-of his tongue. In conversations, comments on the news alternated with reports which emigrants asked of each other about roads, villages, little settlements stuck up in the steepest part of the mountains, inaccessible, unheard of places—so they could go there to leave their families. . . . It seemed that a single family had reunited there. Everybody talked to everybody else with complete confidence. People lent each other help.[8]

Warnings about the imminent arrival of the *Carrancistas* had not in-duced the campesinos to rally behind the *Zapatistas*, who had been se-curing the borders with between 5,000 and 10,000 soldiers. The ordinary people of Morelos were enjoying a peace they had not seen since before 1911 and a harvest superior to any in some years, and they saw little need to fight until things became desperate. The heavy-handedness of the *Carrancistas* practically forced people to embrace *Zapatismo*, as it was the only acceptable option, the other two being death or deportation. Thus, many men returned home after securing their families' safety and joined Zapata. As one villager put it, "I said to myself, 'Rather than have them kill me sitting, standing or walking, I'd better get out of here.' And so I went to war along with the *zapatistas*."[9]

Zapata had also retreated to the hills after his headquarters fell, but he soon established a base of operations at Huautla, a village in the most southern area of the state. At this point, a little more than a month after Cuernavaca's fall, the *Zapatistas* were gathering their forces together, preparing for the resistance that they were to mount in the coming months, a resistance that González already considered dead, quite probably because of the virtual silence of the *Zapatista* guns. Overconfident in his achievement, in early May, González informed Obregón, who had been appointed Carranza's secretary of war, that the rebellion in Morelos had been defeated. (Considering it would ultimately take González another three years to kill Zapata, his boast seems arrogant.) Zapata was also uncertain about the *Zapatistas'* ability to carry on. Indeed, Zapata's dejection over the situation he and his men faced became visible soon after he fled Cuernavaca. While resting at San Vicente on his way back to his mountain headquarters, he reportedly told his soldiers, who were themselves visibly disheartened, "If you don't want to fight any more, then we'll all go to the devil! What do you mean, you don't want to fight?" They were silent, and he went on, "Bah!" he said. "Then there's nothing I can do."[10]

At the beginning of July, a few weeks after Zapata had been forced to retreat from Tlaltizapán, the *Zapatistas* went back on the offensive. Their days of acting as a genuine army, however, were over. Outnumbered and outgunned, the *Zapatistas* would have had no chance against González's forces in a conventional fight. Zapata thus revived the guerilla tactics that he had employed at the beginning of the revolution, when Díaz was the enemy, deploying small units of 100 to 200 men, avoiding engaging the *Carrancistas* in set battles, and launching surprise attacks. The tactic enabled the *Zapatistas* to achieve many successes right from the start of the renewed hostilities, even if those successes were by necessity followed by retreat. In July alone, the *Zapatistas* destroyed garrisons at Santa Catarina and Tepoztlán, massacring the troops stationed in them. They followed those attacks with raids on the Federal District, where military supplies were seized in Milpa Alta, and confronted González at Tlaltizapán, engaging the *Carrancistas* in a seven-hour battle. González, realizing that his forces were ill-equipped to defeat such tactics, issued a manifesto on July 9, warning that he would "proceed with especial severity against all the state's pueblos," if they continued supporting Zapata, and threatening them "with summary punishment without right of appeal."[11]

González's frustration quickly showed, displaying itself, for instance, with Mrs. King, who hounded him about rebuilding her hotel and at whom he snapped, "'This is no time to talk of reconstruction, Señora King! The work of destruction is not yet completed. Will you not comprehend, *señora*, I am about to destroy what still remains of Cuernavaca!' He went on talking," King continues, "saying that there was no stamping out Zapata because all the towns and villages roundabout sheltered the *Zapatistas* in their need; so that he was going to sack them all, including Cuernavaca, and thus run his fox into the open. . . . 'But our homes! Our property!' I cried. 'Oh, *señora!*' he said, almost angrily. 'That is of the past. That is all over.'"[12] González was not simply destroying Morelos for the sake of defeating the *Zapatistas*. He looted as much of the property—factories, haciendas, and other structures—as he could. "Even the huge copper vats in distilleries were melted down and the metal sold,"[13] the historian Ronald Atkins observes, and Mrs. King recalled "all the bathtubs from the Bella Vista . . . 'had been confiscated [and sold], as I had deserted my home,'"[14] and such was the fate of the things in all homes, rich or poor, that had been abandoned, a word whose meaning came to include forcibly evacuated. Consequently, the *Carrancistas* came to be known locally as *los consusunaslistas* (those with their fingers ready), a homonymic play on *los Constitucionalistas*. While ineffective as a means of controlling Morelos, the looting boosted González's personal fortune. As Vicente Blasco Ibáñez observed, González enriched himself: "According to his enemies, in his youth Don Pablo González was a peon in a factory at $20 a month. To-day he is considered one of the richest men in Mexico, both in real estate and personal property. How did he work the miracle? By becoming a General."[15]

González's threats proved as futile as the threats that had been made during the times of Huerta's and Robles' occupations. Those who were fighting for Zapata were in the hills, not in the villages, and therefore difficult to capture. Innocents were the ones who suffered, and the more who did, the larger the *Zapatista* force grew. On August 10, Zapata issued another manifesto, encouraging the people in their opposition but also calling attention to, and seeking to correct, a problem among his own chiefs. Most of them fought hard, but some of them did not fight with the rigor that was needed, either failing to return to or retiring from battles too quickly, and often they took advantages of their positions to steal from the villages, acting no better than González. Condemning such chiefs as "cowards or egoists . . . who have retired to live in towns or camps, extorting from the pueblos or enjoying wealth they have taken over in the shadow of the revolution,"[16] Zapata declared that those who had not taken up arms against the enemy or who retreated without authorization would be discharged dishonorably from the Liberating Army and be required to relinquish their arms, troops, and staff. Lorenzo Vásquez, Zapata's friend from before the revolution and a trusted chief thereafter, went first. Under suspicion of not being loyal after criticizing Palafox in late 1915 and early 1916, he was accused of retreating to quickly from Tlaltizapán and of sympathizing with Pacheco. He, therefore, was proclaimed "unfit to form part of the revolutionary forces, in virtue of his notorious cowardice."[17] Those who proved their bravery, by contrast, were rewarded. When Vázquez was dismissed, Eduardo González, a chief stationed in the Juchitipec area, was promoted to Brigadier General.

Zapata photographed with a large group of his associates. (Library of Congress Prints & Photographs Division, LC-DIG-ggbain-1539)

The guerilla campaign proceeded so well over the summer that, on October 1, Zapata publicly declared, "There is not a single line of communications which it can be said is controlled by *Carrancismo*."[18] This was an exaggeration meant to draw attention to Carranza's failure to crush the opposition, and Zapata drove home his point by launching attacks on sites near Mexico City. The first attack occurred on October 4, when 1,000 *Zapatistas*, which was quite a large number of men to make up a single unit during this period of the revolution, seized the Xochimilco pumping station, which supplied Mexico City with water. The next attack was on San Ángel, a suburb only eight miles from downtown Mexico City. Zapata would continue to order raids outside Morelos throughout October, coordinating attacks in the states of Puebla, Hidalgo, Michoacán, Guerrero, Oaxaca, as well as Mexico State. The objectives were usually such highly visible targets as railway lines, factories, or mills. The point of the attacks, besides obliging Carranza to focus resources on places other than Morelos, was to draw the attention of foreign representatives to the instability of the country under Carranza, in the hope that Carranza's government would lose international recognition. Closer to home, Zapata continued to spur his men to action, holding up Eduardo González and Valentín Reyes, who staged raids two or three times a week, as exemplary. He also continued to implore his chiefs to avoid alienating the population, not only by treating them fairly but also by coming down hard on banditry, a practice that had become a particularly strong temptation, given that the men no longer received pay. The *Zapatistas* continued to gain ground during the last few months of 1916, bringing more and more villages under their control.

González soon grew desperate, increasing the brutality that he had unleashed. "Never did anyone believe," a *Zapatista* secretary, Juan Espinosa Barreda, complained, "that there would be ruffians who surpassed Huerta . . . pueblos completely burned down, timber leveled, cattle stolen, crops that were cultivated with labor's sweat harvested by the enemy . . . to fill the boxcars of their long trains and be sold in the capital . . . Robles damned a thousand times is little in comparison."[19] The *Zapatistas'* attacks grew more spectacular. On November 7, for example, they blew up a southbound train near Joco station, killing four hundred people, soldiers and civilians included.

For days later, González ordered that anyone caught aiding the *Za-patistas*, a charge that included being captured on the roads or near railways without papers or explanation, be shot without trial. Trains continued to be blown up. González was incapable of defending them, and his forces got even more thinly stretched when his men were overcome by a number of diseases. Those suffering illness were both useless soldiers and easy targets. A dysentery epidemic that was caused by famished *Carrancistas* eating mangoes, for example, helped a commander in the north of the state finish off several of them: "[W]hile they were stretched out, [he] went in and just had to take aim and *zas, zas*, he finished them. That's why they named him General Mango." Meanwhile, the spread of malaria in Yautepec brought down so many soldiers that "[t]he streets were full of corpses."[20] By the end of the month, González was preparing for withdrawal.

With González in retreat, Zapata reestablished his Tlaltizapán head-quarters and held back on his operations outside Morelos so that he could ensure that the *Carrancistas* left Morelos. On December 1, the *Zapatistas* launched simultaneous attacks against garrisons in 11 major towns, including Cuernavaca, and by the end of the month, the enemy was pulling out of the region as fast as it could. The *Zapatistas* kept the pressure on, attacking government forces in important towns into January. González's campaign had failed. The *Zapatistas* once again took control of the entire state of Morelos, though a few Constitutionalist troops would remain in the region until the end of February. Now Za-pata's confidence soared, and he declared in a manifesto on January 20, "the nightmare of *Carrancismo*, running over with horror and blood, is at its end."[21] González would not acknowledge his failure until July 7, after months of attempting to acquire the means to stage a counterof-fensive and feeding anti-*Zapatista* stories to the Mexican papers. Before his arrival in Morelos, González had held the distinction of being the only *Carrancista* general who had yet to win a battle. Now he had be-come the *Carrancista* general who proved unable to hold a state with a force that dramatically outnumbered his enemy's.

The cost of the victory, as well as of the defeat earlier in the year, had been high for Morelos. The *Carrancistas* used heavy artillery as they rooted the *Zapatistas* out of the towns; González destroyed prop-erty when he looted the region, and the *Zapatista* insurgency ransacked haciendas for materials to sustain the war effort both before and after González's occupation. The damage caused by the last year of fighting left the state in a shambles, and recovering from the destruction would take time. For instance, in Cuernavaca, where Mrs. King returned in 1916 after a two-year absence, there were "[b]lack, battered, bullet-pierced walls where had been comfortable, happy homes; bridges destroyed, approaches to the town cut off; everywhere signs of the dreadful conflict that had taken place. . . . We drove down the silent streets past abandoned, deserted houses; not a soul in sight. A dog, nosing in a heap of rubbish, slunk away at our approach, and the clatter of the wheels awoke strange echoes in the emptiness. In the heart of town."[22] Even Zapata was shocked by what he witnessed, remarking in a letter he wrote to a secretary upon his return to the state capital after González's withdrawal, "They've left Cuernavaca unrecognizable, the houses are without doors, the streets and the plaza converted into dungheaps, the churches broken open, and the holy images destroyed and stripped of their vestments."[23]

NOTES

1. Other regions were as difficult to control as Morelos. For example, in Chiapas, as in Morelos, the *Carrancistas* kept the towns under their control but not the countryside. Carranza, however, showed much greater concern for Morelos, as is evidenced by the number of troops he sent there to suppress the *Zapatistas*. For an overview of the unrest Mexico faced in the south for the remaining years of Carranza's rule, see Alan Knight, *The Mexican Revolution*, vol. 2 (Lincoln: University of Nebraska Press, 1990), 381–92.

2. Quoted in Robert P. Millon, *The Ideology of a Peasant Revolution* (New York: International, 1995 [1969]), 29.

3. Quoted in John Womack, *Zapata and the Mexican Revolution* (New York: Vintage Books, 1970 [1968]), 250.

4. Friedrich Katz, *The Life and Times of Pancho Villa* (Stanford, CA: Stanford University Press, 1998), 817.

5. Adolfo Gilly, *The Mexican Revolution*, trans. Patrick Camiller (New York: New Press, 2006), 224.

6. Quoted in Womack, *Zapata and the Mexican Revolution*, 250.

7. Samuel Brunk dates the beginning of the negotiations as December (see *Emiliano Zapata! Revolution and Betrayal* [Albuquerque: University of New Mexico Press, 1995], 188), but other historians, for example Womack, date their beginning in February (see *Zapata and the Mexican Revolution*, 251), the month that de la O discovered their existence.

8. Quoted in Gilly, *Mexican Revolution*, 379–80.

9. Quoted in Oscar Lewis, *Pedro Martínez: A Mexican Peasant and His Family* (New York: Random House, 1964), 91.

10. Ibid., 101.

11. Quoted in Roger Parkinson, *Zapata: A Biography* (Briarcliff Manor, NY: Stein & Day, 1980 [1975]), 223.

12. Rosa E. King, *Tempest over Mexico: A Personal Chronicle* (New York: Little Brown, 1940 [1935]), 298.

13. Ronald Atkin, *Revolution: Mexico 1910–20* (New York: John Fay, 1970), 303.

14. King, *Tempest over Mexico*, 302.

15. Vicente Blasco Ibáñez, *Mexico in Revolution*, trans. Arthur Livingston and José Padin (New York: E. P. Dutton, 1920), 77–78.

16. Quoted in Womack, *Zapata and the Mexican Revolution*, 261.

17. Quoted in Brunk, *Emiliano Zapata!*, 191.

18. Quoted in Parkinson, *Zapata*, 224.

19. Quoted in Womack, *Zapata and the Mexican Revolution*, 268.

20. Quoted in Lewis, *Pedro Martínez*, 102.

21. Quoted in Parkinson, *Zapata*, 226.

22. King, *Tempest over Mexico*, 288.

23. Quoted in Brunk, *Emiliano Zapata!*, 194.

Chapter 10

BEYOND THE 1917 CONSTITUTION

Carrancismo, despite its failure in Morelos and Zapata's assertions about its impeding end, remained strong. Unlike when Zapata predicted the downfall of Huerta's government, there was no opposition with nation-wide appeal for Carranza to struggle against. Dissent existed, including that which led to quickly repressed labor strikes in Mexico City, but no political movement capable of putting forth a viable alternative to the Constitutionalists emerged. The *Felicistas*, headed by Felix Díaz, who had returned to Mexico in the summer of 1916 and who was well-funded by conservative Mexicans living in exile in New York, offered a possibility. The group competed against the *Zapatistas* as the most dominant resistance movement in the south, but its reactionary nature was unlikely to find lasting support in the peasant population. Villa also remained an annoyance in the north, waging a guerrilla-style war that occasionally proved dangerous, but he never found the kind of success that the *Zapatistas* were able to achieve. His major triumph was a raid on the city of Chihuahua in September 1916, when he released prisoners from the jail and seized military supplies as well as food. Villa's ability to gather the forces to stage that raid was facilitated by the U.S. presence in the country. This situation brought him support because he was the target of U.S. forces, and he took advantage of anti-American sentiment, attempting to consolidate the resurgence of his appeal. For example, he published a manifesto in October that called for the seizure of foreign owned companies, which was probably read as code for U.S. companies at the time: it "ended with the slogan 'Mexico for the Mexicans.'"[1] Such attempts to mobilize the populace behind him notwithstanding, Villa never gained the strength he had earlier in the revolution. He remained an ineffective challenge to *Carrancismo*.

Carranza, after establishing the Constitutionalists in Mexico City for good, proceeded with his political agenda. Among the most significant items on that agenda was assembling a Constitutional Congress. It was through the establishment of a new constitution that Carranza wanted to secure his legitimacy. Elections for delegates in every Mexican state, with the exception of Morelos, were held in October, and they convened in Querétaro on December 1, 1916, just as Zapata was gaining the upper hand in his battle against General González. Carranza opened the Congress by presenting his version of a new constitution, displaying his presidential status even though he was not yet using the title. The very act of holding the congress, therefore, contributed to legitimizing his rule, but the timing of the convention was also beneficial to Carranza in that it helped him convince the United States to withdraw from the north. Wilson's administration feared that the U.S. presence would embolden the conference to push a leftist agenda. That concern—along with the realization that the United States would soon need to commit troops to Europe, where World War I was raging—pressured the United States into coming to an agreement with Carranza, and U.S. forces began to pull out of the country on January 2. No U.S. troops would be in Mexico by the time the new constitution was ratified, removing the issue Villa was trying to use to rally the populace behind him.

The Constitutional Congress also created problems for the *Zapatistas* in unexpected ways. Although its delegates were willing to work with Carranza, their politics were not always in line with his. Indeed, some were ideologically closer to Zapata and Villa than they were to Carranza. Among the more radical delegates was the Pueblan Luis T. Navarro—a *Maderista* who had joined the *Zapatistas* when Huerta took power—and he defended Zapata's position on agrarian reform, arguing, "When each inhabitant of the Republic has his home and his piece of land to cultivate, the causes of revolution in our fatherland will have been eliminated."[2] Navarro's participation in the land-reform debate, which was not started until late January, near the end of the congress, was instrumental in helping the more radical delegates get a land reform provision, Article 27, incorporated into the final draft of the new constitution. The provision, which Navarro felt did not go far enough, established that property ownership was not an individual right and that land distribution should be determined by the public good, giving legitimacy, in effect, to the pueblo system that Zapata had been fighting to save. Zapata's ability to claim the moral high ground was weakened: people could point to the constitutional land reform provision to justify putting down their arms or deciding not to take them up and keep the fight alive.

The constitution was ratified on February 5, and elections were announced for March 11. Carranza stayed out of Mexico City, campaigning for the presidency around the country, even though he was running unopposed. With another impending election guaranteed to be won by his enemy, Zapata was again concerned that a government that he could not recognize would have a real claim to legitimacy, both nationally and internationally. Unable to directly influence international opinion, Zapata set out to demonstrate to the nation that the *Zapatistas* were the only source of true land reform. Having secured Morelos's borders in February, creating a defense that deterred González from even attempting to renew hostilities, Zapata instituted a village-centered approach to government and land distribution, one that was codified by a law passed in March. That law not only gave villages the power to distribute land as their custom said it should be distributed but also established the rules of military behavior for those in the Southern Liberating Army. They were now forbidden from interfering in village politics or land-distribution policies and from seizing "village or ex-hacienda land, since no individual, whether an officer or not, has a right to more than the land-area distributed to him."[3] The villages were even given the power to determine what their relationship would be with the *Zapatistas*, who had reestablished a central government in Morelos with its own departments—including departments of agriculture, education, justice, and war—along the lines of the shadow government that had been in place under the Convention banner in 1915.

The government that was being established for Morelos differed in some respects to the one that the *Zapatistas* had advocated earlier in the revolution. In the beginning, when land redistribution was carried out by revolutionaries in defiance of the governments in Cuernavaca and Mexico City, all actions had to be approved by headquarters—although, later on, officers in the field were empowered to make decisions. In both cases, the *Zapatista* central authority were sanctioning the activities. The reliance on such an authority became more obvious once the *Zapatista* Convention came into being, although village councils and the documents that they held to demonstrate villages' rights were involved in the process so that land was distributed as particular villages thought fit. The more decentralized nature of the 1917 law deemphasized the authority of the *Zapatista* government and thus stood in stark contrast to the one that was established by the new constitution. Mexico's government was to be centralized in the extreme, placing the most power in the office of the president—more power, in fact, than the president had held during Porfirio Díaz's years of dictatorship, for Carranza's constitution eliminated the vice-presidential office and weakened the legislature. The pace and the nature of the land reform that the constitution promised would be determined by the president, that is, Carranza, who had won the March 11 election and been sworn into office on May 1—though the vote was not unanimous, as Obregón and González received write-in votes despite their not having campaigned. In fact, Carranza had only allowed Article 27 of the Constitution to remain because it gave the president the authority to levy taxes on, or even seize, foreign-owned oil and mining companies.

Zapata marked Carranza's inauguration with the publication of "Protest to the Mexican People," a manifesto in which he argued that Carranza's election had not been democratic but a "cynical and brutal imposition."[4] At this point, however, Zapata had more to worry about than Carranza. Tension was undermining the unity of *Zapatismo*, despite the *Zapatistas'* regaining the upper hand in Morelos. At the beginning of May, for example, a revolt against the Tlaltizapán authority broke out in Buena Vista, a village near Anenecuilco, and Zapata, as well as de la O, traveled there with troops to put it down. Fierce fighting between the *Zapatistas* and the traitors went on for days. A wealthy resident of Buena Vista, discussing the *Zapatistas*, explained,

"The truth is they are devils. Who can guess how many are dead? I didn't know what a volley really was. It is frightful! Are they dogs? If one fell, the others went right over him. We couldn't even take aim without trembling with fear."[5] The episode showed that even those closest to Zapata could not be fully trusted. The revolt had been organized by Lorenzo Vásquez, who had been with the *Zapatistas* since 1911; he felt underappreciated and complained to Montaño. Montaño was also discontented by this point because he had long been displaced as a central figure in the *Zapatista* organization by Palafox. The two discussed abandoning Zapata and joining the *Carrancistas*, and Vásquez was apparently in the process of doing so when the fight broke out at Buena Vista. Shortly thereafter, he was hung as a traitor, and Montaño was soon implicated in the affair by some of Vásquez's men. Montaño stood trial for treason, was found guilty after two days of testimony, and was sentenced to death on May 17, 1917, for conspiring against Zapata. He was sent before a firing squad the following day, and his body was hung next to Vásquez's. Zapata was deeply hurt by the defection of his friend, who maintained his innocence until the end, and could not bear to watch the proceedings against him. Zapata thus left Tlaltizapán before Montaño had been arrested, instructing Palafox: "with regard to any crime other than treason, this Authority will concede the favor of a pardon, but for the mentioned crime of treason, today as always I am disposed to deny such a favor."[6]

The following month, Zapata suffered a more personal loss. His brother Eufemio, who had grown more volatile under the stress of fighting a war with no end in sight, had become more unpredictable, particularly when drunk. One old man, the father of a *Zapatista* chief, Sidronio "Loco" Camacho, failed to take into account that problem one day when Eufemio was drinking in Cuautla, where he was again stationed. Eufemio, in a drunken rage, proceeded to insult and then beat the old man to death. The following day, June 19, Camacho arrived in Cuautla and shot Eufemio, throwing him, still alive, onto an anthill outside of town to prolong his suffering as he lay dying. Camacho then defected, seeking and receiving amnesty from Carranza and thereby preventing Zapata from extracting his own revenge. Understanding the justice of his brother's fate, about which quite a few people were not unhappy, Zapata was, nonetheless, profoundly affected. He began to isolate himself and show the frustration he was suffering—a frustration that had manifested itself as early as 1916—in a much more pronounced form. "His normally taciturn character," a young guard wrote from headquarters, "had become dark, crabbed, irascible, somewhat neurasthenic, to the point that even the men of his escort feared him when he called."[7]

Despite the darkening of his mood, Zapata found someone in whom to place his hope: Gildardo Magaña, whom Zapata had met when he was in Mexico City in 1911. Magaña had arranged to have the Plan de Ayala published in Mexico in December of that year and now rose to greater prominence, becoming Zapata's most trusted advisor. Magaña had already gotten close enough to Zapata to urge him to seek allies among *Carrancista* commanders and others outside the *Zapatista* movement, something Zapata had become wary about doing because his previous attempts to forge alliances with such outsiders as Orozco and Villa had failed to produce the desired results. Magaña's status as a trusted outsider—someone not from Morelos who had not betrayed the revolution—persuaded Zapata to allow Magaña to see what he could accomplish, and after Eufemio's death, Zapata stepped up his diplomatic efforts. He had begun to realize, it seems, that achieving success through diplomacy was the best option available to him if he had any hope of exerting an effective and lasting influence on the country's future agrarian policies. Before long, Palafox lost his influence, coming to serve as a messenger between Magaña and Zapata. Palafox attempted to escape the indignity of his fall by negotiating a surrender with Carranza and promising to bring a host of *Zapatista* intellectuals with him in exchange for being allowed to go into exile. Zapata discovered Palafox's betrayal before it could be executed, and for the latter half of 1917 and for most of 1918, Palafox—who was not executed because Magaña advised against the idea, fearing that killing another central *Zapatista* figure would undermine the credibility of *Zapatismo*—remained in the *Zapatista* camp as little more than a prisoner.[8]

The first figure with whom Magaña seriously began to negotiate was not an outsider but a Puebla chief and former *Zapatista*, Domingo Arenas. He had signed an accord with Carranza at the end of 1916 but now suggested that he repented defecting. Arenas was possibly attempting to take control of the southern revolution from Zapata, whose forces he was depleting with the help of money and other supplies. Arenas, in any case, delayed declaring that he had rejoined the *Zapatistas*. A conference between him and Magaña, at which the problem was to be sorted out, was held at the end of August near Tochimilco. A shoot-out erupted, the cause of which is not known for certain, and Arenas was killed, either by Magaña, in hand-to-hand combat according to some reports, or by a sniper in the armed escort that Magaña had brought with him. Some commentators assume Zapata ordered Arenas, whose body was displayed as a trophy, killed. Others claim the gun battle broke out when he tried to convince Magaña and the other *Zapatistas* at the conference to join Carranza, or when he demanded that he be made the head of the revolution.[9]

Looking beyond this failure when he returned to camp, Magaña urged that the diplomatic process be continued, and efforts were made to reestablish contact with Villa and Emilio Vásquez Gómez, to whom Zapata personally wrote, asking him in vague terms to keep fighting for the cause. *Carrancista* figures, including Lucio Blanco, who was living in exile in Texas, were sought out as potential allies as well, yet Zapata also issued a "Manifesto to the Nation" on September 1, 1917, that differentiated *Zapatistas* from *Carrancistas* and *Felicistas*. Denouncing Carranza as a pseudo-revolutionary, the manifesto declared that the only true revolutionaries were fighting for the principles of the Plan de Ayala. That the manifesto emphasized the notion of the plan's "principles" rather than just the plan was important, for such wording indicated that the spirit of the document was more important than an exact adherence to it. The wording also showed that Zapata was willing, as his delegates had been at the Aguascalientes Convention, to be realistic about implementing the plan. The *Zapatistas*' perceived inflexibility over getting their allies, both actual and potential, to stick to the plan, after all, had hindered Zapata's ability to negotiate in the aftermath of Huerta's defeat. The new manifesto was thus, in some respects, a sign of Zapata's desire to be less rigid with potential allies as well as a demonstration of his unwillingness to compromise on his core ideals.

As Zapata's and Magaña's diplomatic efforts continued, the *Carrancistas*, now constitutionally the *federales*, began preparing for an attack on Morelos, surrounding the state with battalions in order to trap the *Zapatistas* in the middle and crush them for good. Under the command of General Cesáreo Castro, who was replaced by González shortly after the campaign began at the beginning of November, the *Carrancistas* made inroads in the state's eastern zone, where Camacho and Cirilo Arenas, Domingo Arenas's brother, led the invasion. They took control of Cuautla on November 19. Over the following two weeks, they captured Jonacatepec and Zacualpan. These early successes created a sense of optimism among *Carrancistas* in Mexico City, and a number of news articles soon proclaimed that the end of the war was near. The war effort went no further, however. Indeed, Carranza was soon facing unrest elsewhere in the country, including in his home state, Coahuila, where a rebellion broke out in protest over voting irregularities. Zapata and Magaña tried to capitalize on the new unrest, but much of it quickly dissipated, although the discontent with Carranza that it revealed did not. Indeed, another sign of Carranza's apparent weakness was the expansion of the *Felicista* movement throughout 1917 and 1918.[10] Zapata and Magaña now looked to form ties with the *Felicistas*, although *Zapatismo* propaganda continued to denounce them, and, at the beginning of 1918, they went so far as to reach out to Carranza, promising him that the *Zapatistas* would recognize his government if it would leave Morelos alone. Carranza ignored the offer.

After a visit from an American, William E. Gates, in early February 1918, Zapata's pursuit of allies began to seem more urgent. Gates had come to Mexico under the guise of doing archeological research, some of which he carried out, but he also wanted to learn about modern Mexico and sought out revolutionary figures to satisfy his curiosity. Styling himself as a sort of envoy from Washington when he came to Morelos, Gates convinced Zapata that a U.S. military intervention would begin after the war in Europe ended if the rebellion did not manage to unify, overthrow Carranza, and establish a lasting peace. Gates actually told Zapata and his advisors, Magaña and others, that Wilson had decided, "if Mexico cannot save herself, she must be saved from herself for herself." Gates, who was summarizing the words he used in his article "The Four Governments of Mexico: Zapata—Protector of Morelos," continued, "Mexico's patriots, have still the right to prove their ability to rebuild her [Mexico]. . . . 'The responsibility in this cause,'" he concluded, "'lies already on your shoulders, and of other Mexican revolutionists, and to avert what will never come if President

Wilson can prevent it, and shall not come if I can tell the story of what I have seen in Mexico well enough to do something to forestall the approach. You need no urging; but I say it: See that Mexico does not make intervention necessary, for her own salvation.'"[11] The specter of a U.S. intervention in the absence of a peaceful Mexico could have re-invigorated the opposition, or at least that is what Zapata hoped. Yet it sometimes worked against him, for, as the historian James D. Cockcroft writes, "the U.S. threat of armed force intimidated many of them [the *Zapatistas*], some of whom laid down their arms and sought amnesty from Carranza."[12]

NOTES

1. Adolfo Gilly, *The Mexican Revolution*, trans. Patrick Camiller (New York: New Press, 2005 [1971]), 225.

2. Quoted in Eberhardt Victor Niemeyer, *Revolution at Querétaro: The Mexican Constitutional Convention of 1916–1917* (Austin: University of Texas Press, 1974), 134. For discussions of Navarro's influence on the debate, see Charles Curtis Cumberland, *Mexican Revolution: The Constitutionalist Years* (Austin: University of Texas Press, 1972), 355, and John Womack, *Zapata and the Mexican Revolution* (New York: Vintage Books, 1970 [1968]), 372–73.

3. Quoted in Gilly, *Mexican Revolution*, 272.

4. Quoted in Samuel Brunk, *Emiliano Zapata! Revolution and Betrayal in Mexico* (Albuquerque: University of New Mexico Press, 1995), 207.

5. Quoted in Oscar Lewis, *Pedro Martínez: A Mexican Peasant and His Family* (New York: Random House, 1964), 108.

6. Quoted in Brunk, *Emiliano Zapata!*, 200.

7. Quoted in Womack, *Zapata and the Mexican Revolution*, 288.

8. For this account of Palafox's brush with a firing squad, see Brunk, *Emiliano Zapata!*, 218–19. Another story relates that Palafox—who had also angered Zapata by criticizing potential allies and who came to be seen as the architect of the failures of 1915—was discredited in a scandal involving his homosexuality. See Womack, *Zapata and the Mexican Revolution*, 306 and Frank McLynn, *Villa and Zapata: A History of the Mexican Revolution* (New York: Carroll & Graf, 2002), 357 for this version of the story.

9. For a variety of accounts of this episode, see David G. LaFrance, *Revolution in Mexico's Heartland: Politics, War, and State Building in Puebla, 1913–1920* (Lanham, MD: Rowman & Littlefield, 2007 [2003]), 190; Timothy J. Henderson, *The Worm in the Wheat: Rosalie Evans and Agrarian Struggle in the Puebla-Tlaxcala Valley of Mexico, 1906–1927* (Durham, NC: Duke University Press, 1998), 62–63; Brunk, *Emiliano Zapata!*, 210; Womack, *Zapata and the Mexican Revolution*, 293; and McLynn, *Villa and Zapata*, 353.

10. For accounts of the expansion of *Felicistas* activities in this period, see Alan Knight, *The Mexican Revolution*, vol. 2 (Lincoln: University of Nebraska Press, 1990), 381–92.

11. William E. Gates, "The Four Governments of Mexico: Zapata—Protector of Morelos," in *The World's Work*, vol. 37 (New York: Doubleday, Page, 1919), 661–62. Womack argues that Gates's discussions led Zapata to increase his diplomatic efforts to unify all the revolutionary factions against Carranza (see *Zapata and the Mexican Revolution*, 299–300), but more recently, Knight has noted that Zapata's attempts to unify the revolution "could have derived from his desperate need for allies" (*Mexican Revolution*, 610), even though Zapata's activities seem to have increased, as Womack shows, immediately after Gates's departure.

12. James D. Cockcroft, *Mexico: Class Formation, Capital Accumulation, and the State* (New York: Monthly Review Press, 1983), 110.

Chapter 11

THE FINAL BETRAYAL

Following his discussions with Gates, Zapata turned to the work of unifying the revolution with more fervor and became more explicit about his willingness to compromise than he had been in his September 1917 manifesto. He now looked to deemphasize the issues that had kept the various factions apart, calling for "the mutual and reciprocal forgetting of all the differences that have divided revolutionaries in the past"[1] in a decree published in March 1918. Around the same time, he released two manifestos. One acknowledged the need to work out the divisions that set Mexicans from different areas of the country apart so that after the revolutionary's success a Mexican government that would address the concerns of all Mexicans could be formed. The other manifesto maintained that differences between groups, specifically between peasants and urban workers, did not necessarily imply that their causes were different: "May the calloused hands of the countryside and the calloused hands of the workshop unite in a fraternal salute of concord because, in truth, if the workers are united we are invincible, we are the force and we are the right: we are tomorrow!"[2]

Such rhetoric was followed up in April with appeals to the *Arenistas*, that is, the forces of the deceased Domingo Arenas, who were now

led by Cirilo Arenas. That month, they had turned on Carranza, who
had attempted to incorporate their forces into the larger Mexican army
and thereby assert more control over them. They would sign an accord
with the *Zapatistas* in May, despite the fact that the *Arenistas* blamed
Zapata for the death of Domingo, who was regarded as a martyr among
his former followers. Negotiations with the *Felicistas* also became more
fluid. Zapata decided, over the objections of Magaña, that ideological
disputes could be ignored and the problems that they created could be
worked out later. The important thing at this stage was to find accord.
Near the end of the month, Zapata published yet another manifesto,
one that was vague in its details but again called for a junta to work out
ideological differences after victory was achieved. He sent this manifesto to the revolutionary leaders, asking them to sign the document as
a show of allegiance to the revolution at large. It was meant to serve as
a pledge of unification.

Throughout the spring and for the rest of the summer, Zapata continued his diplomatic efforts at home. He renewed his drive to find
international support, particularly working to get his voice heard in
Washington, asking Francisco Vásquez Gómez—whom he thought
might get more results than his mouthpiece, Octavio Paz Solórzano,
had been able to get—to take up his cause. Closer to home, Zapata
had to contend with the defection of Morelos's population, which was
becoming less inclined to aid the *Zapatistas* and more willing to accept Carranza's government as its own. Things had gotten so bad that
Zapata, who retained the respect he had been accorded since the days
of Madero's presidency, became personally involved with securing the
support of villagers. He, for example, traveled to particular villages as
early as February 1918 to handle dissent among the people. They had
set up defense forces with the approval of Zapata but were now as likely
to raise their weapons to turn away *Zapatistas* as they were to protect
their territory from *Carrancistas* or other threats. The leaders of these
community forces sometimes considered themselves the true *Zapatistas*. One of them, recalling the role he felt he had assumed during this
period, observed, "It was not the government but 'we, the *Zapatistas*
ourselves, who re-established order' in Morelos."[3]

Zapata soon concentrated his attention on Obregón, who had resigned from Carranza's administration after the passage of the consti-

tution and whose discontent with the president was becoming more public. In July, the *Zapatistas* issued "A Toast to Álvaro Obregón," a leaflet praising Obregón for speaking out against the government. Zapata followed up on the toast with two letters, which he sent directly to Obregón in August. Trying to build upon the earlier manifesto, the one in which he had equated the working class with the peasant class—a manifesto that had been a subtle way to reach out to Obregón, one of whose sources of support was the working class—Zapata stressed the commonality of the peasants' and workers' causes. He suggested that these causes were, or should be, Mexico's:

> That the revolution of the country represents the interest of the majority and that of the towns points out the procedure for the rectification and dignifying of the Mexican Indian, no one can deny. It is also beyond question that the city revolution is founded upon powerful agents of progress, who are inevitably connected with the problem of improving the status of the depressed working classes. The fundamental error . . . in all our action since 1915 consists in our two forces having remained divided and in conflict. . . . Here is the explanation for our not having been able to establish peace in our country. . . . Why not unify the Revolution? . . . Why not accomplish this patriotic act of brotherhood and accord if it will serve to eliminate the spurious element of personalism?[4]

Obregón was uninterested in joining Zapata and simply ignored his advances. Indeed, Zapata had very little to offer by the summer of 1918, having been weakened considerably. The *Carrancistas*, it is true, had made little progress in Morelos, remaining confined to the areas of Cuautla and Jonacatepec, but they had not really attempted to expand their operations in the state, focusing their energies on the *Felicistas*, who now seemed the more potent threat.

The situation for the *Zapatistas* would soon change for the worse. The fall brought a bad harvest and the Spanish influenza, which, along with malaria, dysentery, and typhus fever, decimated the undernourished population of Morelos. By the end of November, the *Zapatistas* were reduced to a few thousand poorly armed men. That month,

González prepared for a new operation in the region and was ready to attack. He held off doing so to avoid exposing his men to the flu. When the rains stopped in December, he was able to take full advantage of the *Zapatistas'* reduced forces and moved into Yautepec, Jojutla, Cuernavaca, and Tetecala without encountering any significant resistance. By the middle of the month, the *Carrancistas* had even taken Tlaltizapán. Rather than repeating the mistakes of his previous occupation of the state, González established garrisons in all its villages and began to reestablish Morelos's economic strength, repairing railways, putting seized haciendas up for rent, and working to repopulate the region by, for example, offering rural laborers free passage to it.

Zapata became little more than a fugitive. He was able to fight occasionally, going out on raids with his men, but he was mostly confined to the safety of the hills, where González's forces could not follow him. Another problem at the time was Palafox. A shortage of men in October had obliged Zapata to use Palafox for a diplomatic mission, and he took the opportunity to escape. The following month, arguing that Zapata was corrupt—more interested in personal gain than in the people of his state—Palafox began urging the *Zapatistas* to abandon the Southern Liberating Army in favor of the agrarian movement that he was establishing. Adding to that threat of defection was General Cesáreo Castro, who offered Magaña, along with others whom Carranza believed could be trusted to put down their arms, an amnesty deal if they would turn themselves in. The *Zapatista* chiefs, despite the dire predicament in which their movement found itself, remained loyal, rebuffing the disgraced Palafox and ignoring Castro, although some soldiers and minor leaders did put down their arms and return home, perhaps giving up the fight altogether or perhaps just ceasing to fight temporarily to wait for conditions to improve.

Palafox's betrayal led Zapata to assess more carefully what had gone wrong with the momentum his movement had won just a few years earlier, and he wrote a history of Palafox's place within it, a history he completed in early January 1919 and that pinpointed the turning point for *Zapatismo* in August 1914. Looking back, Zapata defines the problem as Palafox's inflexibility during negotiations with *Carrancistas*. Zapata, of course, had supported Palafox at the time, but with the *Zapatistas* in the worst shape they had seen themselves in since turning on

Madero, Zapata would only confess to not reigning in Palafox and making a deal with some key Constitutionalists when he had a chance. The Convention government may have then succeeded, but the time to negotiate had passed long ago. Zapata had only a weak hand with which to play, and Carranza no longer needed to even sit down at the table, as he had realized a year earlier when Zapata had offered to recognize Carranza's government if it would allow Morelos to govern itself. By 1918, Carranza wouldn't even extend an offer of amnesty to Zapata.

In the meantime, attempts to forge alliances went on. In January of 1919, Zapata gave up his pretensions to being the revolution's primary leader, a role conferred upon him by the Plan de Ayala, and granted that distinction to Francisco Vásquez Gómez. The change was announced on February 10 and illustrates the import Zapata was giving to accommodating *Zapatismo* to other movements. Trusting Vásquez Gómez, after all, suggested that Zapata was now willing to compromise on land reform rather than just remain vague about what he was willing to give up for the sake of unity, as he had been doing up until this point, and then insist at a later date that his plan would be followed, for Vásquez Gómez's views on social reform gave very little emphasis to the land issue. The agreement with Vásquez Gómez may also have been another response to Palafox's charge that he was corrupt, for it certainly demonstrated that Zapata was not seeking personal gain or power. Naming a new revolutionary chief, however, caused difficulties elsewhere. Manuel Peláez, for example, would not accept Vásquez Gómez as the leader because he wanted that position for himself, and Peláez was an important part of the *Zapatistas'* strategy. He came from a family of landowners in Mexico's oil-rich gulf coast region and had earned the support of U.S. oil companies in his fight against Carranza, whose desire to seize oil fields troubled international observers. Securing Peláez as an ally offered the *Zapatistas* a chance to bring to their movement money, guns, and international support. Alienating him was, therefore, something to worry about, but the bigger problem was finding a way to accommodate the interests of various revolutionary factions.

On March 17, still facing difficulties securing signatures on his unification manifesto, Zapata published an open letter to Carranza. Rejecting the legitimacy of his presidency and addressing him as a mere citizen—one whose concern for Mexico should have compelled him to change the course that he had been following—Zapata accused Carranza of forgetting the purpose of the revolution: "It never crossed your mind that the revolution should be for the benefit of the broad masses, for the immense legion of the oppressed whom you and yours roused up with your speeches. . . . For you to triumph, however, it was necessary to proclaim grand ideals, to affirm principles and to announce reforms."[5] The letter also served as another attempt to win over Obregón, for it called attention to the fact that the concerns of the peasantry and the working classes had not been adequately addressed by the present government and argued that the success of the revolution should incorporate the needs of both groups, granting liberty to their members. But mere words had little chance of changing the course of the revolution. Zapata needed to restore the military prowess that he had enjoyed back in 1914 and 1915. Around the time that his open letter was published, he was presented with a chance to do so.

A rift between González and a colonel named Jesús Guajardo offered Zapata the opportunity to secure a potent ally—one who could supply weapons and men—and regain some momentum in Morelos. He wrote to Guajardo, inviting him to join the *Zapatistas*. Reaching out to Guajardo was yet another sign of the growing desperation of the *Zapatistas*, not because of the unlikelihood of a *Carrancista* joining the *Zapatistas* but because Guajardo was remembered for his cruelty during González's first occupation of Morelos: "In Cuautla it was hell; it stank from so many dead," one peasant recalled. "They gathered us together with the cattle—there were about four hundred head—and Guajardo took them away; we could only get back twenty-five. Then we went away to the *cerros* [that is, the hills] to live like animals."[6] He was a representative of the very thing the *Zapatistas* were fighting, but Zapata had to take the opportunities that presented themselves. Whether or not Guajardo would have accepted the invitation cannot be known. González intercepted the letter and almost immediately began planning a trap to capture and kill Zapata. Guajardo, under González's orders, accepted Zapata's invitation. Zapata, aware of prior assassination attempts, was cautious. He asked Guajardo, on April 1, to demonstrate his commitment to the *Zapatistas* by attacking the *Carrancistas*, particularly Victoriano Bárcenas, a former *Zapatista* chief who was not only perpetrating cruelties upon the people of Morelos but also upon those closest to

Zapata. He had, for example, arrested Gregoria Zúñiga, one of Zapata's mistresses, as well as her and Zapata's child, María Luisa.

Guajardo stalled, probably to give himself the time to prepare a believable ruse, although one that allowed all the targets to remain alive was not found. Bárcenas's men were attacked on April 9. Some were killed immediately, and another 59 were captured and executed. Zapata was convinced that Guajardo could be trusted. Later in the afternoon of the ninth, the two met near Jonacatepec. Zapata, who brought around 30 men to the meeting, was presented with a horse called *As de Oros* (Ace of Gold). Then the two made arrangements to travel to Chinameca hacienda to retrieve the munitions Guajardo had promised. They set out later that night: Zapata stopped on the road along the way to sleep, while Guajardo went on to Chinameca. Early in the morning on April 10, Zapata went forward, meeting Guajardo outside the hacienda and discussing future military action in Morelos. Later, responding to rumors that González's troops were in the area, Zapata left with 30 men to assess the threat, which proved not to exist. He returned about noon and was invited inside but dawdled for another half an hour. Then, after discounting warnings that Guajardo couldn't be trusted, he prepared to join his prospective ally:

> "We're going to see the Colonel and I want only ten men to come with me," [Zapata ordered]. He rode toward the gate of the hacienda. Ten of us followed him as he had ordered, while the rest waited full of confidence under the shade of the trees with their carbines in their cases. A squad, lined up in formation, seemed ready to pay him honors. Three times the bugle sounded the salute of honor, and as the last note faded away and as our commander in chief appeared at the threshold of the gate, the soldiers who had presented arms fired their rifles twice at point-blank range in the most treacherous, cowardly, and vile manner, not giving us any time to reach for our pistols, and our unforgettable General Zapata fell, never to rise again.[7]

Zapata was dead. Falling for Guajardo's trick seems an uncharacteristic mistake for Zapata, whose cautious nature had served him well for so many years. But finding opportunities to infuse his movement with some life had become urgent, leaving him with little choice but to trust in Guajardo, who would not have been the first officer to abandon the *federales* for the *Zapatistas* because of a personal dispute. Diplomacy, after all, was proving a slow process and those with whom Zapata was in contact couldn't be relied upon, while changing the momentum of his resistance might have given him a stronger hand in any future negotiations. In any case, without the aid of Guajardo or someone like him, there seemed to be very little hope. Thus Zapata took his chances and embraced the rallying cry with which he reportedly began the revolution: "it is better to die on your feet than to live on your knees."[8]

Zapata must not have been completely surprised when the end came. He had hoped that if he died his memory would reinvigorate the *Zapatistas* and the revolution at large, a topic he is said to have discussed the night before he was killed. Over dinner, he reportedly discussed with his men the power that martyrs have for the movements they represent. His death does seem to have restored the faith some peasants had in him. One recalled, "I was on my way back from Guerrero [where he had fled to avoid the destruction González had inflicted on Morelos in 1916], when the news of Zapata's death came. . . . It hurt me as much as if my own father had died! I was a *Zapatista* down to the marrow of my bones. I had a lot of faith in Zapata's promise, a lot of faith."[9] Such reactions did not translate into action.[10] In the aftermath of the ambush, the *Zapatistas* were in disarray, not exactly sure about what they would do next. It would take some months to restore any sense of cohesion to their resistance.

Guajardo, by contrast, immediately began the process of publicizing his success, throwing Zapata's corpse over a mule and bringing it to Cuautla, where the body was put on public display the following day. Photographs that were taken the night Guajardo arrived in the town were soon printed in the national newspapers so that the image would be available for all to see. Exhibiting the corpse was an attempt, it seems, to prove that Zapata was dead. González even showed some skepticism at first, readying his men in case Zapata had killed Guajardo and was coming to Cuautla to stage a surprise attack. But even with the public display, many would not believe that Zapata had been killed. The corpse, locals claimed, lacked Zapata's distinctive birthmark, as well as a facial mole, and possessed the little finger Zapata was said to

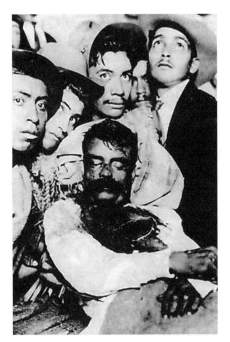

Postmortem portrait of Zapata, Cuautla, 1919. (El Universal via Getty Images)

have lost. Reported sightings of Zapata riding his horse in the mountains of Guerrero would follow, though some in the state maintained that he had left the country, taking up exile somewhere in the Middle East. Outside Morelos such rumors had little power, and Carranza and his supporters sought to take control of the significance of Zapata's death by announcing the death of *Zapatismo*. Following the public viewing in Cuautla, numerous articles about Zapata's demise appeared in the Mexico City press. Many of these were simple hype that sought to justify Guajardo's methods and demonstrate his bravery.

Despite their disarray, the *Zapatistas* could not sit still and allow Carranza to conduct a propaganda war unopposed. So, on April 15, they published their own perspective on Zapata's death, yet over the next few month, the *Zapatista* leaders could not agree on who should take Zapata's position. When Magaña became the official leader at the end of the summer, he secured his position with a vote that was held in the absence of some of the most important *Zapatistas*, including de la O, who was also seeking to take Zapata's place. Unity had not been found, and the problem got worse when Magaña surrendered to Carranza in

November, taking a number of chiefs with him. *Zapatismo* again seemed to be close to extinction, and Magaña's rejoining of the group at the start of the following year served only to confirm the divisions that had emerged during the summer. De la O was particularly adamant about rejecting Magaña's leadership, and the two separately joined Obregón's uprising against Carranza later in 1920.

Obregón's ascent to the presidency effectively ended *Zapatismo*, but not its aspirations. Obregón's government and those that followed it, in order to help crush dissent, incorporated Zapata's story into the official revolutionary narrative, sanitizing his opposition so that in later years Zapata would be able to sit, however ironically, next to Carranza, as well as others whom he rejected, in the pantheon of revolutionary heroes. Zapata thus came to be betrayed by the official revolutionary narrative, as much as he was by Guajardo, and by the second half of the 20th century, Zapata, the people's revolutionary, lost some of the power he held as a symbol, even though agrarian movements that opposed the government and were sometimes violent did call upon the memory of Zapata to legitimize their causes. Still, he was generally regarded as a symbol of the establishment. In 1968, for example, his image had become so tied to the government that anti-government student protestors did not reject Zapata as a symbol but never even considered using him; as one protestor noted, "I never thought of Zapata as a student symbol, an emblem. Zapata has become part of the bourgeois ideology; the PRI [Partido Revolucionario Institucional (Institutional Revolutionary Party)], has appropriated him."[11] But more recently, Zapata has begun to reemerge as a symbol of the oppressed, serving that function for the revolutionaries of Chiapas in the mid 1990s, who took the name of his movement for their own and proclaimed "Zapata is in all of Mexico. Zapata is not dead; he is alive and will live forever."[12]

NOTES

1. Quoted in Samuel Brunk, *Emiliano Zapata! Revolution and Betrayal in Mexico* (Albuquerque: University of New Mexico Press, 1995), 213.

2. Robert P. Millon, *The Ideology of a Peasant Revolution* (New York: International, 1995 [1969]), 107.

3. Quoted in Alan Knight, *The Mexican Revolution*, vol. 2 (Lincoln: University of Nebraska Press, 1990), 368.

4. Quoted in Millon, *Ideology of a Peasant Revolution*, 107. Original translation slightly modified.

5. Quoted in Jonathan Fox, *The Politics of Food in Mexico: State Power and Social Mobilization* (Ithaca, NY: Cornell University Press, 1993), 44.

6. Quoted in Arturo Warman, *"We Come to Object": The Peasants of Morelos and the National State*, trans. Stephen K. Ault (Baltimore: John Hopkins University Press, 1980 [1976]), 131.

7. Quoted in Enrique Krauze, *Mexico: Biography of Power; A History of Modern Mexico, 1810–1996*, trans. Hank Heifetz (New York: HarperCollins, 1998), 303.

8. Quoted in Frank McLynn, *Villa and Zapata: A History of the Mexican Revolution* (New York: Carroll & Graf, 2002), 90.

9. Quoted in Oscar Lewis, *Pedro Martínez: A Mexican Peasant and His Family* (New York: Random House, 1964), 108.

10. Memories like the one recorded here may also be revisionist reconstructions: see Samuel Brunk, *The Posthumous Career of Emiliano Zapata* (Austin: University of Texas Press, 2008), 46–48.

11. Quoted in Eric Zolov, *Refried Elvis: The Rise of the Mexican Counterculture* (Berkeley: University of California Press, 1999), 127.

12. Quoted in José Rabasa, *Without History: Subaltern Studies, the Zapatista Insurgency, and the Specter of History* (Pittsburgh, PA: University of Pittsburgh Press, 2010), 47.

APPENDIX

The following poem—with a prose translation by Albert and Maria Raquel Rolls—attests to the interest that ordinary Mexicans had in Zapata, an interest that was likely heightened by the news of his death, and illustrates the ambiguity of Zapata's reputation. His character is lauded but his death, the poem concludes, will hopefully bring peace and allow Morelos to develop its economy again, suggesting that Morelos's problems had continued into 1919 because Zapata had lived until that year. It was published in an undated broadside that was sold for five cents, probably not too long after Zapata's funeral, by the printing house of Antonio Vanegas Arroyo, who died in 1917 but whose business was carried on by his son. Incidentally, Vanegas Arroyo's print shop played an important part in fashioning the 20th-century image of Zapata. It was the employer of José Guadalupe Posada (1852–1913) who illustrated penny newspapers sold in Mexico City until his death and was the first to create artistic representations of Zapata. "Later, his prints of Zapata were models for Diego Rivera's and José Clemente Orozco's paintings of this revolutionary figure."[1]

Pormenores del Entierro de Emiliano Zapata

Vengo de Cuautla Morelos
he llegado a Amecameca,
Y traigo de Chinameca
Un negro crespón de duelo

¡Quien no conoce a Zapata!
Aunque sea en fotographia
Que era un hombre que valía
Lo que pesaba y en plata

Muchos su causa tomaron
Pensando de buena fe,
Mas después se descarriaron
Y su descrédito fué.

Quien peleó por el derecho
Y la santa Libertad,
Vió su ideal todo deshecho
Y rodeado de Maldad.

Las hordas de bandoleros
A su bandera acogidos,
Eran tan solo bandidos
A caza de los dineros

Guajardo era un carrancista
Que tenía mucha inventive,
Mucho tacto y mucha vista
Y de voluntad activa.

Al señor Pablo González,
Ofrecio acabar la lata
Que desde los federales
Les venía dando Zapata

Y combinando un buen plan
Púsole la trampa al zorro
Y calló sin más ni más
Como si fuera un Cachorro

Su cádaver fué enterrado
El sábado once de abril
Y al panteón acompañado
Por dolientes más de mil.

Sus parientes asistieron
Y altos jefes militares
Y a su fosa lo siguieron
Las gentes de esos lugares

Todos lloraban en coro
Lamentando aquella muerte
Comentando en triste lloro
Su tan desgraciada suerte

Triste es mirar que entre hermanos
Se cometan tales cosas
En vez de dares las manos
Para empresas laboriosas.

Esperamos; pues, en Dios
Que muerto ese jefe audaz
Al extinguirse su voz
Renazca la ansiada paz.

Murió Emiliano Zapata
Que causó tantos desvelos
Vuelva el trabajo y la plata
Al estado de los Morelos.

DETAILS OF EMILIANO ZAPATA'S FUNERAL

I have just arrived in Amecameca, having come from Cuautla, Morelos, and I bring from Chinameca my black mourning clothes. / Who doesn't know Zapata, a man who was worth his weight in silver, if only through pictures of him? / Many took up his cause in good faith, but after they went astray, it was discredited. / He who fought for the people's rights and holy freedom saw his entire ideal wasted and surrounded by evil. / Hordes of bandits took up his flag, but they were just bandits looking for money. / Guajardo, a very inventive and tactful *carrancista*, had good sight and active intentions. / He offered *señor* Pablo González a chance to put an end to the trouble that Zapata had been causing the *federales*. / And arranging a good plan, he laid his trap and shut Zapata up just like that, as if he were a puppy. / His body was accompanied to the cemetery by more than a thousand mourners and buried on Saturday, April eleventh. / His relatives, as well as senior military leaders, attended, following him to the grave. / Everybody was crying in chorus, regretting his death and sadly commenting on his bad luck. / It is sad to see such things happen among brothers instead of seeing them join their hands for business. / We hope, therefore, in God that the death of that brave *jefe* and the extinction of his voice revives the desired peace. / Emiliano Zapata, who caused many sleepless nights, died. Come back work and money to the state of Morelos.

NOTE

1. Jacqueline Barnitz, *Twentieth-Century Art of Latin America* (Austin: University of Texas Press, 2001), 9.

SELECTED BIBLIOGRAPHY

Atkin, Ronald. *Revolution: Mexico 1910–20*. New York: John Fay, 1970.

Barnitz, Jacqueline. *Twentieth-Century Art of Latin America*. Austin: University of Texas Press, 2001.

Blasco Ibáñez, Vicente. *Mexico in Revolution*. Trans. Arthur Livingston and José Padin. New York: E. P. Dutton, 1920.

Boyd, Lola E. "Zapata." *Américas* 20, no. 9. (September 1968), 2–7.

Brenner, Anita, and George R. Leighton. *The Wind That Swept Mexico: The History of the Mexican Revolution of 1910–1942*. Austin: University of Texas Press, 2008 [1943].

Brunk, Samuel. *Emiliano Zapata! Revolution and Betrayal in Mexico*. Albuquerque: University of New Mexico Press, 1995.

Brunk, Samuel. "The Mortal Remains of Emiliano Zapata." In *Death, Dismemberment, and Memory: Body Politics in Latin America*, ed. Lyman L. Johnson, 141–78. Albuquerque: University of New Mexico Press, 2004.

Brunk, Samuel. *The Posthumous Career of Emiliano Zapata*. Austin: University of Texas Press, 2008.

Coblentz, Stanton Arthur. *The Militant Dissenters*. London: A. S. Barnes, 1970.

Cockcroft, James D. *Mexico: Class Formation, Capital Accumulation, and the State*. New York: Monthly Review Press, 1983.

Creelman, James. "President Díaz: Hero of the Americas." *Pearson's Magazine* (March 1908), 231–77.

Cumberland, Charles Curtis. *Mexican Revolution: The Constitutionalist Years*. Austin: University of Texas Press, 1972.

Dunn, Harry H. *The Crimson Jester: Zapata of Mexico*. New York: R. M. McBride, 1934.

Eisenhower, John S. D. *Intervention! The United States and the Mexican Revolution, 1913–1917*. New York: W. W. Norton, 1993.

Ferguson, Hayes. "Zapata Symbolizes Failure: Much of Mexico Still in Poverty." *Times-Picayune* (July 8, 1998), A1, http://www.lexis-nexis.com/.

Fox, Jonathan. *The Politics of Food in Mexico: State Power and Social Mobilization*. Ithaca, NY: Cornell University Press, 1993.

Fyfe, H. Hamilton. *The Real Mexico*. New York: McBride, Nast, 1914.

García, Mario T. *Luis Leal: An Auto/Biography*. Austin: University of Texas Press, 2000.

Gates, William E. "The Four Governments of Mexico: Zapata—Protector of Morelos." In *The World's Work*, vol. 37. New York: Doubleday, Page, 1919.

Gilbert, Dennis. "Emiliano Zapata: Textbook Hero." *Mexican Studies/ Estudios Mexicanos* 19, no. 1 (Winter 2003), 127–59.

Gilly, Adolfo. *The Mexican Revolution*. Trans. Patrick Camiller. New York: New Press, 2006.

Gonzales, Michael J. *The Mexican Revolution, 1910–1940*. Albuquerque: University of New Mexico Press, 2002.

Hart, Paul. *Bitter Harvest*. Albuquerque: University of New Mexico Press, 2005.

Haslip, Joan. *The Crown of Mexico: Maximilian and His Empress Carlota*. New York: Holt, Rinehart and Winston, 1972.

Helm, MacKinley. *Mexican Painters: Rivera, Orozco, Siqueiros and Other Artists of the Social Realist School*. Mineola, NY: Courier Dover, 1989 [1941].

Henderson, Peter V. N. *In the Absence of Don Porfirio*. Wilmington, DE: Scholarly Resources, 2000.

Henderson, Timothy J. *The Worm in the Wheat: Rosalie Evans and Agrarian Struggle in the Puebla-Tlaxcala Valley of Mexico, 1906–1927*. Durham, NC: Duke University Press, 1998.

Hind, Emily. "Historical Arguments: Carlos Salinas and Mexican Women Writers." *Discourse* 23, no. 2 (Spring 2001), 82–101

Hodges, Donald C., and Ross Gandy. *Mexico, the End of the Revolution*. Westport, CT: Praeger, 2002.

Independent 82, no. 34670 (May 17, 1915), 275.

Information Annual, 1915. New York: R. R. Bowker, 1916.

Jiménez, Carlos M. *The Mexican American Heritage*. 2nd ed. Austin: University of Texas, 1994.

Johnson, William Weber. "Zapata: A Conservative Old Red." *Life* 66, no. 7 (February 21, 1969), 16.

Jowett, Philip S., A. M. De Quesada, and Stephen Walsh. *The Mexican Revolution, 1910–20*. New York: Osprey, 2006.

Katz, Friedrich. "The Agrarian Policies and Ideas of the Revolutionary Mexican Factions Led by Emiliano Zapata, Pancho Villa and Venustiano Carranza." In *Reforming Mexico's Agrarian Reform*, ed. Laura Randall, 21–35. Armonk, NY: M. E. Sharpe, 1996.

Katz, Friedrich. *The Life and Times of Pancho Villa*. Stanford, CA: Stanford University Press, 1998.

Katz, Jesse. "The Curse of Zapata." *Los Angeles Magazine* 47 (December 1, 2002), 102–5, 176–79.

King, Rosa E. *Tempest over Mexico: A Personal Chronicle*. New York: Little Brown, 1940 [1935].

Knight, Alan. *The Mexican Revolution*. Vol. 2. Lincoln: University of Nebraska Press, 1990.

Krauze, Enrique. *Mexico: Biography of Power: A History of Modern Mexico, 1810–1996*. Trans. Hank Heifetz. New York: HarperCollins, 1998.

Kropotkin, Peter. *Evolution and Environment*. Ed. George Woodcock. Montreal: Black Rose Books, 1996.

LaFrance, David G. LaFrance. *Revolution in Mexico's Heartland: Politics, War, and State Building in Puebla, 1913–1920*. Lanham, MD: Rowman & Littlefield, 2007 [2003].

Lewis, Oscar. *Pedro Martínez: A Mexican Peasant and His Family*. New York: Random House, 1964.

McLynn, Frank. *Villa and Zapata: A History of the Mexican Revolution*. New York: Carroll & Graf, 2002.

McNeely, John H. "Origins of the Zapata Revolt in Morelos." *Hispanic American Historical Review* 46, no. 2 (May 1966), 153–169.

Moats, Leone B. *Thunder in Their Veins: A Memoir of Mexico*. New York: Century, 1932.

Newell, Peter E. *Zapata of Mexico*. Montreal: Black Rose, 1997.

Niemeyer, Eberhardt Victor. *Revolution at Querétaro: The Mexican Constitutional Convention of 1916–1917*. Austin: U of Texas P, 1974.

Parkinson, Rogers. *Zapata: A Biography*. Briarcliff Manor, NY: Stein & Day, 1980 [1975].

Preston, Julia and Samuel Dillon. *Opening Mexico: The Making of a Democracy*. New York: Farrar, Straus and Giroux, 2005.

Quirk, Robert E. *The Mexican Revolution, 1914–1915*. New York: W. W. Norton, 1970 [1960].

Rabasa, José. *Without History: Subaltern Studies, the Zapatista Insurgency, and the Specter of History*. Pittsburgh, PA: University of Pittsburgh Press, 2010.

Ragan, John David. *Emiliano Zapata*. New York: Chelsea House, 1989.

Revolutions in Mexico: Hearing Before a Subcommittee of the Committee on Foreign Relations, Senate Committee on Foreign Relations, 66th Congress, 1913.

Ross, Stanley Robert. *Francisco I. Madero: Apostle of Mexican Democracy*. New York: Columbia University Press, 1955.

Sanderson, Steven E. *Agrarian Populism and the Mexican State: The Struggle for Land in Sonora*. Berkeley: U of California P, 1981.

Simpson, Lesley Byrd. *Many Mexicos*. Berkeley: University of California Press, 1967 [1962].

Starr, Frederick. *Mexico and the United States: A Story of Revolution, Intervention and War*. Chicago: The Bible House, 1914.

Testa, David W. Del. "Zapata, Emiliano: Mexican Revolutionary, 1879–1919." In *Government Leaders, Military Rulers, and Political Activists*, ed. David W. Del Testa et al., 202. Westport, CT: Greenwood, 2001.

Vargas Llosa, Alvaro. "History of the Mexican Revolution Shows Why Migration Continues Today." *Desert Morning News* (November 7, 2007), http://www.lexis-nexis.com/.

Wallace, David Foster. "E Unibus Pluram." In *A Supposedly Fun Thing I'll Never Do Again*, 21–82. New York: Little Brown, 1997.

Weinberg, Bill. *Homage to Chiapas: The New Indigenous Struggles in Mexico*. London: Verso, 2000.

Werstein, Irving. *Land and Liberty*. New York: Cowles, 1971.

Warman, Arturo. *"We Come to Object": The Peasants of Morelos and the National State*. Trans. Stephen K. Ault. Baltimore: John Hopkins University Press, 1980 [1976].

Womack, John. *Zapata and the Mexican Revolution*. New York: Vintage Books, 1970 [1968].

Zolov, Eric. *Refried Elvis: The Rise of the Mexican Counterculture*. Berkeley: University of California Press, 1999.

WEBSITE

Plan de Ayala. Trans. John Womack. http://www.hist.umn.edu/~rmccaa/la20c/ayala.htm.

INDEX

About the Author

ALBERT ROLLS, Ph.D., teaches at Touro College in New York City. He has written a biography of Stephen King and a study of Shakespeare, as well as co-edited H. W. Wilson's *World Authors 2000–2005* and other biographical reference works.